THE ADIRONDACKS

Photo by Chester D. Moses & Co.

AVALANCHE PASS

The Adirondacks

T. Morris Longstreth

PRINTED FROM THE 1917 ORIGINAL

ILLUSTRATED WITH
PHOTOGRAPHS AND
MAPS

BLACK · DOME

Published by

Black Dome Press Corp.
1011 Route 296, Hensonville, New York 12439
www.blackdomepress.com
Tel: (518) 734-6357

First Edition Paperback 2005
Copyright © 2005 Black Dome Press Corp.

All rights reserved.

The Adirondacks was originally published in 1917
by The Century Co., New York.

ISBN: 1-883789-44-3

ISBN: 978-1-883789-44-2

Library of Congress Cataloging-in-Publication data is available.

Front cover: Photograph of Little Cherry Patch Pond
© by Nathan Farb, from *Adirondack Wilderness*, 2005,
available at nathanfarb.com. Used with permission.

Cover design by Ron Toelke Associates

Printed in the USA

10 9 8 7 6 5 4 3 2 1

DEDICATED, WITH AFFECTION

TO

THOMAS K. BROWN
OUR ONE-TIME MASTER,
OUR OFT-TIME COUNSELOR,
OUR ALL-TIME FRIEND.

Lynn.
&
Morris.

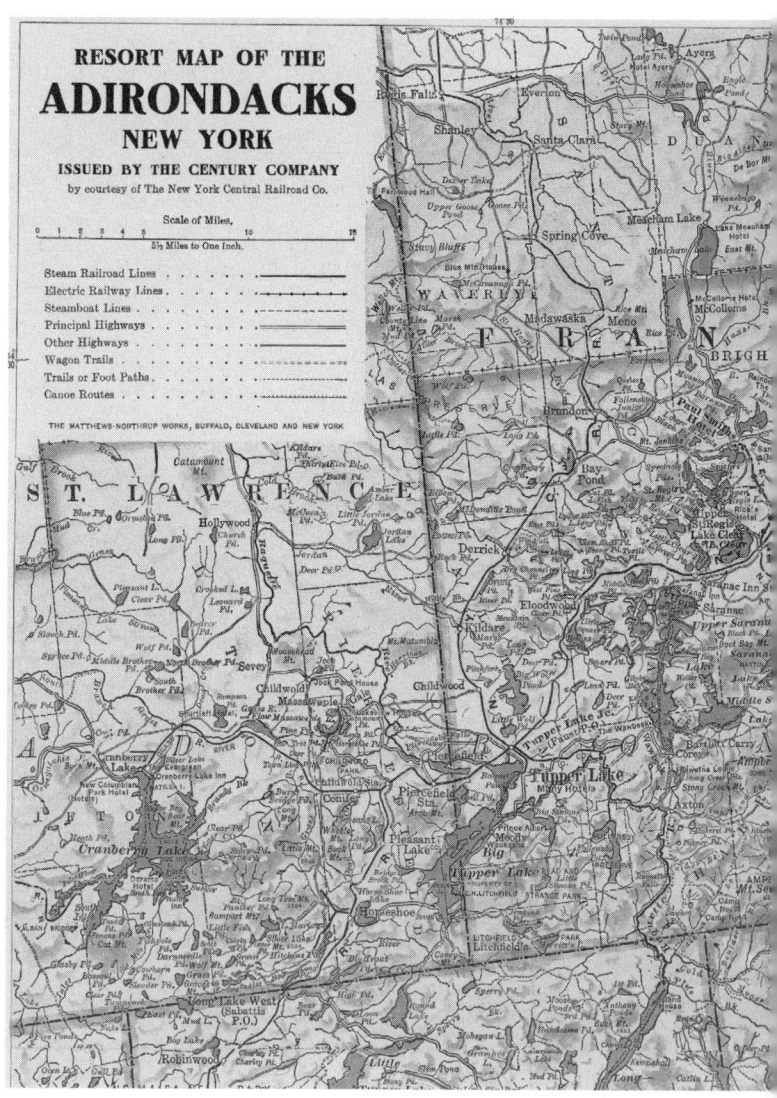

MAP

THE ADIRONDACKS

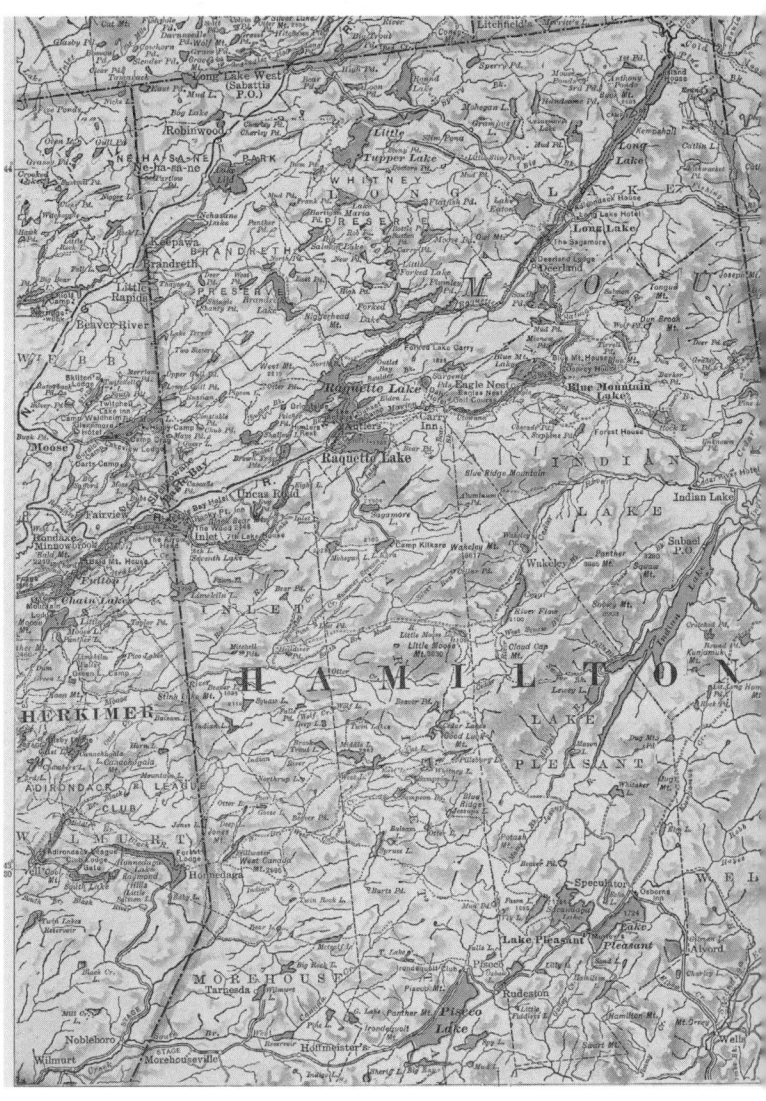

MAP

INTRODUCTION

"But on the Raquette the nights are just as mysterious, the spruce-lands just as alluring, the spell of the twilight just as subtle, the wandering odors just as sweet as in more distant wildernesses. Go see for yourself."

T. Morris Longstreth

Any Adirondack explorer who has ever vacationed in the west runs the risk of never wanting to come back. Once you have seen those rocky peaks pocked full of glaciers and snowfields, why would you care to look upon our rounded foothills ever again? Who that has walked through a high alpine meadow under a sun unfiltered by haze can bear to go back to our overwooded, rarely sunny bump-on-the-map here in northern New York? How can our eastern mountains compare with the grand ranges of the western landscape?

Or more to the point, how could a travel writer fresh from sampling those western spectacles describe the Adirondacks faithfully, without making his readership prefer to go to the Rockies instead?

This was exactly the dilemma faced by T. Morris Longstreth when he sat down to write his 1917 travelogue, *The Adirondacks*.

The previous year, he had set out with his childhood friend Lynn and his "little Western horse,"

INTRODUCTION

Luggins, for a six-month tour of the Adirondacks. The expedition began at the North Creek rail station in June and would end at the same location just before the final onset of winter in December. With the memories of superlative adventures in Wyoming and Montana still fresh in their minds, Longstreth experienced doubt as soon as he saw the "trifle bulgy" hills lining the upper Hudson River. He explained: "… from the memories of a youthful trip I had drawn upon my comrade's credulity to the point of making a summer of it in the Adirondacks. And now the Adirondacks did not rise to the occasion."

What *had* attracted them to the region was its sheer size. At that time, Adirondack Park was only 3.3 million acres, roughly half of its current size, and yet it was still larger than any of the more breathtaking parks they had visited out west. By Longstreth's reckoning, the state-owned Forest Preserve accounted for nearly half of the park's open space, but since many private landowners were once again welcoming campers—"the natural hospitality has returned to stay," Longstreth was happy to report—the entire region was essentially one big wilderness playground.

They were not in the woods very long, however, before Lynn and the author were completely won over by the beauty of the Adirondacks' lakes and trout streams. "Whoever has heard the whitethroat in some remote valley," Longstreth says, "or the hermit thrush from the deep wood at evening has been bound with invisible strings to the wilderness." He then defends the modest features of the landscape against comparison with the "natural extravagances" of the west, as he calls them. Here there are neither extreme heights of mountains nor extreme depths of canyons, just the haunting lakes and the balsam forests—an endless wilderness into which "the bewildered man" may find ways to lose and starve himself to death "were his heart set on it."

Thus Longstreth, with his well-traveled perspective, comes to view the Adirondacks as an immensely accessible and hospitable wilderness, readily available to millions but known intimately by very few.

Having been bitten with an earnest appreciation for their surroundings, Lynn suggests that their trip needs an underlying motive to press them to further and further explorations—that is, to write the type of guidebook that had not been written on the region (by his own estimation) in many years. And while the book that Longstreth did write may not have been quite as encyclopedic as his friend had hoped, it did not fall far short of that vision, either.

In reality, Longstreth's literary tendencies probably needed very little encouragement. It is quite evident that he was fond of literature—*The Adirondacks* is rife with allusions to Shakespeare and other classics—and that he was a prolific writer in his own right. His subsequent publications are too numerous to list here, but *The Adirondacks* was followed a year later by *The Catskills*. He also published *The Laurentians: The Hills of the Habitant* in 1922 and *The Silent Force: Scenes from the Life of the Mounted Police of Canada* in 1928, suggesting the scope of his travels and interests.

A large portion of his published work would be devoted to young adult fiction, with throwaway titles such as *Coins and Crossbones* (1925) and *Showdown* (1950). However, it is his travelogues for which he will undoubtedly be best remembered, and where his talents were most plainly evident. When Lynn planted that idea in his mind, he was onto something.

While all but the final chapters of *The Adirondacks* are told in the first person, Longstreth provides few biographical clues about himself. He refers to his youth several times, and indeed he was thirty that year. He is clearly affluent enough to take a six-month sabbatical—longer, when one considers that he spent three months the very next spring to make a 400-mile trek across the Catskills in preparation for his next travelogue—and well-connected enough to be socially acceptable at the Lake Placid Club, even in his flannel woods clothes. But besides these clues, he offers few details about himself. His storytelling abilities effectively divert the reader's attention to the woods and waters at every turn, preserving the privacy of the storyteller himself.

Perhaps it doesn't enhance the reader's appreciation of *The Adirondacks* to know that its author was a schoolteacher from Kingston, New York, at the time, or that nearly forty years later he wrote a well-remembered, scathing critique of J. D. Salinger's *The Catcher in the Rye*. The reader, after all, is looking for adventure, of which Longstreth is generous in the portions he serves. There are all the episodes which we as readers demand and expect of any Adirondack storyteller, including tales of battles with black flies, trout tempted to the surface of wild streams, and of evening loon song over darkening lakes. We also have flashes of backwoods ingenuity, such as the mad attempt to float Luggins across Dead Creek Flow on a raft.

What Longstreth really provided us, however, is a snapshot of what it was like to visit and explore Adirondack Park in 1916, just before the United States declared war on Germany. In this aspect, his lucid and often wry observations of people and places really shine. He tells of the uneasiness he felt passing the "uninhabited clearings" on the trail to Kings Flow; the hospitality of camp owners on Little Moose Lake; a bore encountered on the trail to Blue Mountain; and the residents at Cranberry Lake whose attitudes towards outsiders mellow significantly after Labor Day. Longstreth admits, however, that he is not a gifted observer of nature, and in this category he defers to other writers he admires.

One episode that stands out from the rest of the book is the party's encounter with the Lake Placid Club. That Longstreth merits inclusion in the club's exclusive society, he is greatly pleased and flattered; but that the club's terms of membership are so skewed as to exclude the vast majority of the human race, he is keenly aware and vaguely disturbed. He sings the praises of this "most original association" and its "energetic and elevating dream," but he takes ironic note of the five classes of humanity to which the club assigns prospective members. He comments finally, without passing judgment himself, "Thanks to the closeness of the unguessed scrutiny and to the superior level of influence demanded, the easy charm of the place has not had to wane with growing numbers."

It was the wild side of the Adirondacks that Lynn and Longstreth came to see, however, and which captured their imagination the most. Having forgotten all about the Rockies, they regretted not having the chance to explore every corner of the Park. In writing an epitaph for their stay at Heart Lake, Longstreth with his peculiar wit summarized the success of the entire trip, and expressed a sentiment that many other campers before and after have shared:

> The first thought instigated by the more enchanting places in the Park was to settle in each one for life. Since that proved inconven-

ient offhand, the next was to promise ourselves an immediate return for that purpose. Consequently there are at least half a dozen localities where we are engaged to spend the rest of our days.

Any modern hiker, sportsman, or camper will identify immediately with Longstreth's experiences. We know at once of the largeness of the woods—and the summer days spent in them—of which he writes, and we have all experienced that "vision of serenity worth far greater struggle to attain" while perched at the precipice of some mountain ledge. Like Longstreth, we know that to carry the health and the simple lifestyle of the woods with us into our everyday lives is "to improve upon content." Longstreth expresses so precisely our own love of the Adirondack wilderness that in the end we feel he knows us much better than we, as the readers of his travels, can ever know him.

Bill Ingersoll

South Trenton, New York
February 2005

Bill Ingersoll is the Wild Lands Stewardship Chair for the Adirondack Mountain Club Conservation Committee. He has published articles in *Adirondack*

Life and *Adirondack Explorer*, and is a monthly contributor to *Adirondack Sports and Fitness*. Since 2003 he has been working with Barbara McMartin in updating and reprinting the *Discover the Adirondacks* series of hiking guidebooks.

FOREWORD

It had been raining for almost ten days, and we were getting short of small-talk, when Lynn made his suggestion.

"Let's look ahead," he said. "We've remembered the sugar and the lantern and the dish-towel, but we've left out the most important thing of all."

"Not matches," I said, "and there's lots of punky dope left. What do you mean?"

"This trip needs an underlying motive," he went on, "or it'll peter out. It's good enough fun fishing, and it's good enough fun getting lost, but it'd be a whole lot better if there was reason for doing these things. I think I've got one!"

I paid more attention to the fire than I did to him, because he's always gratifying his passion for making good things better, while I like to gratify mine for letting them alone. But he stopped spitting on the little whetstone with which he was putting a double-extra-fine edge on his ax and began again:

"Did you ever see a book on the Yellowstone Park?"

"Dozens. Why?"

"Well, this Park's bigger, but did you ever see one about it?"

I thought a moment, but couldn't remember having seen anything of the sort.

"You haven't," he went on, "because there isn't such a thing. You can read whole book-shelves on the south pole, and Liège, and other places you can't visit, but there's nothing about this Park as it is now, and I bet you, out of the forty million people who live around here—"

"Oh, come now, forty million!"

"Yes, forty million within a five-hundred-mile circle of this spot, and not forty thousand of them know that these forests and mountains and fish and things we're enjoying for nothing are here for them to enjoy also for nothing."

"Aren't you glad?" I said. "It would be awfully crowded, for they would all come if they knew. But I don't see how that supplies our trip with an ulterior motive?"

"We'll write a book," he exclaimed. "I'll study the map and chop the wood, and all you'll have to do is put down the necessary words. It'll make us do the country thoroughly."

I rebelled, but in vain.

For the next two days it rained steadily, and we kept to camp. Lynn's idea germinated, and like the Arab's camel, took possession of the tent. We planned out a tour that left no stone undescribed.

It proved a rainbow summer, but the marvel of it was that, at the end, we should find a pot-o'-gold publisher. I suspect it was Lynn's thirst for thoroughness that did it. All along he kept insisting that the book should be more than a record of our wanderings, spacious though they were. He wished for an

Adirondack Arkeology, a treatise that should treat generously of every topic from aborigine to zoo. No type of reader was to turn from its pages disappointed.

My hope is more modest. I hope there may be some reader besides myself to turn from them at all. After the reality, they paint so palely the wilderness colors and breathe so thinly of the good wood-smells that Luggins himself never would take a second sniff.

One word more, and the Park shall speak for itself. There are but two kinds of travelers; those who enjoy the road, and those who think they shall have enjoyment at the end of it. To the latter pass the time of day good-naturedly enough, but reserve the former for your company. And now, when I would come out from between the lines to speak of my friend, I cannot, for at any moment he may come to read over my shoulder. This I can say, however. Luggins loves him, too, and I never met a horse, I here and now declare, who enjoys better sense.

T. MORRIS LONGSTRETH.

Camp Fellows',
July, 1917.

TABLE OF CONTENTS

CHAPTER		PAGE
	FOREWORD	
I	AN ABORIGINAL APPROACH	3
II	NORTH CREEK TO CHIMNEY MOUNTAIN	26
III	WE TRAVEL NORTH BY SOUTH	46
IV	THE CEDAR RIVER COUNTRY	64
V	THE ADIRONDACK FOREST	80
VI	THE RAQUETTE RIVER TRIP	102
VII	UNCONSIDERED CRANBERRY	143
VIII	ANIMALS OF THE ADIRONDACKS	173
IX	THE GOSPEL ACCORDING TO PAUL SMITH	208
X	LAKE PLACID AND AN EXPERIMENT IN INTELLIGENCE	231
XI	THE GIANTS CLOTHED WITH STONE	258
XII	A CHAPTER OF ENDS AND ODDS	297
XIII	WINTER PREFERRED	303
XIV	WEATHERING THE WEATHER AND THE FLY	318
XV	ON HERMITS AND OTHER TRAGEDIES	333
XVI	THE SPIRIT OF THE PARK	344
XVII	DUFFLE	352
	INDEX	367

LIST OF ILLUSTRATIONS

	FACING PAGE
Avalanche Pass	*Frontispiece*
Southwest from Pharaoh Mountain	18
Forest Cover: Brant Lake Country	35
North from Pharaoh Mountain	54
A Legal Lean-to for State Land	71
An Adirondack Lumber Camp—30° below	81
Pines of Saranac	96
The Three Minute Tent	105
Nameless Creek	116
Log Drive on the Raquette River	125
The Long Lake Country	135
Road House of the Old Staging Days	146
Indian Pass Brook: The Infant Hudson	156
Hanging Spear Falls of the Opalescent	165
South from the Summit of Indian Pass	176
Midsummer Mildness	185
The First Reinforced Concrete	196
Ausable Chasm	205
The Peak of McIntyre from Tahawus' Top	216
Mt. Colvin and Sawtooth (right) from the Ausable Club	225
The Ausable River	236
Tahawus, Algonquin and Iroquois; The Great Range	245

ILLUSTRATIONS

	PAGE
Lower Ausable Lake	256
Sawtooth from the Upper Ausable Lake	265
Indian Pass from Lake Henderson	276
Keene Valley from Keene Heights	285
Crown of the Cloud-Cleaver	296
The Original Winter Sport	305
Whiteface in November from Cobble Hill . . .	316
A Home of the Old Wolf Days	325
How Doth the Hermit	336
The Spirit of the Park	345

THE ADIRONDACKS

CHAPTER I

AN ABORIGINAL APPROACH

HERE and there among the epic groupings of scenery upon our planet one chances upon a little lyric landscape and ever afterward cherishes it. When one comes to consider the matter, it all at once seems strange that upon a surface as extensive and as varied as this, there should be so little domestic scenery,—if that be the term for what is neither wild nor commonplace.

Certain of the counties of England have just the proper cadence and color to recommend them to this class of countryside, but where else in localities of equal extent can you find it? The truth is that nature abhors a vacuum only a little more violently than she eschews a happy medium. For the most part, her mountains are too high, her oceans too big, her plains too excessively plain.

In our own country there is such an example of natural extravagance that there might be found in the lay of the land some palliation for the national fault. Our smallest unit is a thousand miles. A little prairie is a pleasant thing, but day after day of it takes on the nature of an extravaganza. A few Rockies here and there add considerably to the view, but ten thousand square miles of splendor is an emotional tax upon any tourist. One needs a little Kansas thrown in.

And so it goes. The Grand Canyon is so unbearably grand, the open ocean so intolerably open, that we soon find nothing to admire in any prospect that is not palpably monstrous. It is nature's own fault if we have been schooled to praise her masterpieces at the top of our lungs and to ignore the rest.

I know a country, however, where there are no Vesuvian smoke-pots, no Himalayan heights, no Samoan trances, no abominable abysses, and yet where there are quiet lakes and haunting vistas that are unutterably satisfying to a man's soul. It is a country where there is sternness, but sternness tempered by a smile; where there is silence, but silence broken by the call of birds. And if this should seem too soft to those who pine for tragic deaths, I would say that there are still spaces, wild and wide enough, wherein the bewildered man might perish of starvation were his heart set on it.

Thus one comes to the Adirondacks, not to

AN ABORIGINAL APPROACH

eulogize, but to enjoy. The spirit of the North Woods differs from the spirit of the other great playgrounds of our land. In the Yellowstone one feels aggrieved if there be not a new wonder every minute. In the Adirondack Park there are no wonders, no grievances. Hot springs, Sequoias, Crater lakes, glaciers,—there are none of these things, not even a desert!

Consequently the professionals keep away. There are no rhinos, and the big-game hunter goes to Africa; there are no chances to fall a mile off a cliff, whereupon the big-mountaineer goes west and the meek inherit the good average earth that he has left. And because there are so few meek, there is plenty of room for everybody.

But in a matter of understanding, there can be no beginning except at the foundation. The region in question first appeared above the sea about five billion years ago. There is, of course, dispute among the daters, but the average guess seems to be about that date if you are inquiring from one who is not too stingy with his periods.

Somewhere, then, in the antiquities of Archæan time, the Appalachians groped and heaved above the waters—the world's first seashore. Swept by great tides and eroded by equatorial torrents, they washed lazily back into the primeval ocean only to make a reappearance as the ages rolled on. This time they stayed. They were the primal ranges,—there were no Alps, no Himalayas, no Rocky Mountains,—and their head, Tahawus, the Cloud-cleaver, was over eight thousand feet high before he stopped growing. Upon his lower slopes the ocean weeds still grew.

Gradually more and more of the future site of the United States came to light. The rains and the frosts beat and chiseled until the granite ledges could withstand no longer, and about the island of mountains spread a rolling plain. To the eastward rose sister heights, and to the south the ranges waved in parallel chains, but there were no connecting ridges. Nothing infringed upon the Adirondack island and its mountains stood as the embodiment of stonish giants,—elevated, grim, alone. But they did not remain grim for long. The pulverized granite deepened and decayed into a bed for seedlings, and vast areas of white pine spread in utter loneliness up to the rounding peaks. There was, however, one spectacular change to come. Due to the infinitesimal but perpetual oscillation of our planet-pendulum, the climate cooled from a white pine to a juniper stage, then to the dwarf-willow stage, next to the stage where winter snow lasted in places through the summer, and finally to the stage where it snowed the summer through. The snows piled up, crushing deep,—five thousand feet, it is thought,—and their gigantic forefoot of ice

AN ABORIGINAL APPROACH

gouged out great valleys, scratched the hardest barriers, and at last majestically retreated. Oh, what a slush there must have been!

Though the ice retreated, it could never put back the valley bottoms, and, behind each terminal moraine, the waters collected. On the hillsides the soil began to accumulate once more; the willow, juniper, and pine returned; the moose and wolves and all their wild clans spread through the wilderness, and one evening of prehistoric calm a signal fire arose, kindled by the first Indian scout. It said, "Come; this land is good hunting!"

Rival tribes saw and obeyed that signal, and so fierce were the contests for the deer run-ways, so murderous the first impulses of the rival braves, that the entire country became known as "The Dark and Bloody Ground." All the way from the Lower St. Lawrence came the Montagnais Indians,—though I cannot conceive why,—and from the south, bands of the Iroquois swarmed into the mountains to repulse them. The Montagnais and other Algonquins were nearly always defeated and had to retreat, leaving their scalps behind them. Neither did they learn to bring enough food from their stores of fish and venison so that, running out of food, they had to provide a precarious vegetarian commissary from the buds of moose-bushes and the bark of other trees. It was this spectacle that roused the Mohawks to derision. They called the Montagnais tree-eaters, which, being translated into Iroquois, means Ad-i-ron-daks.

Thus we come to the jest that names our greatest eastern park-land; only we have substituted the dining-table for the diner. However, the mountains are a monument to those who fared less well than they; and the last laugh is again best, for the derisive Mohawks are remembered by an inconsiderable river, while the derided Montagnais cannot be forgotten while the most lovely mountainland endures. Other members of the ungentle Iroquois, the Oneidas and Onondagas, were also accustomed to forage on the Adirondack slopes, and they were as keen as the Mohawks to fall upon visitors from the North in this scenic slaughter-house. Villages grew on its outskirts, but, within the confines of the mountains, the frequent massacres prevented all settlements. All was dark and roving and the tomahawk never rested in a truce.

But there was a day coming when the savages could no longer pursue their bloodshed with undiverted satisfaction. It came in 1609, and from two directions. With but the flapping of a mainsail, as the little *Half Moon* hove to at the place to be known as Beverswyck, Fort Orange, and afterwards, Albany, these Indians could not be expected to be much excited. They killed a tasty

AN ABORIGINAL APPROACH

dog to make a Dutchman's holiday, and they could not be expected to foresee that the off-spring of their guests would drive them back toward their diminished preserves. Their medicine men predicted none of the startling events that the same summer already had witnessed further north.

Near the ruins of Fort Ticonderoga is an old rock, cleft from the mountain, which is called Split Rock to this day. This marked the ancient domain of the Algonquin from the Mohawk. But on a certain day in July, a fleet of war canoes, filled with painted Algonquins and accompanied by a Frenchman who looked very much like William Shakspere, crossed the boundary, moving south. They were met at twilight off the promontory that was afterward to see so much of the fortunes of war, and, secure in their new war-magic, waited till the dawn. The Mohawks attacked, but the new French fire-arms had the final word.

It is strange that the word of this encounter in July had not tempered the hospitality shown Hudson in September; but the Englishman sailed down his river without knowing how far he was from China, the port of his endeavor, and without guessing how near he was to his great contemporary and national rival who also was bent on going cross lots to Kubla Khan.

With firearms and new reasons for rivalry, the

differences between the northern and southern wildernesses grew more sharp. The Mohawks were so enraged at the alliance of their old enemies with France that when the pale faces made their way up from New Amsterdam and when the English later sought their aid, they were ready to give it. There is no reason to doubt that it was the few shots fired by Champlain that later lost New France to Saxon rule.

While Indians and whites were swarming up and down the Lake-that-is-the-Gate-of-the-Country, there was very little encroachment upon the Adirondacks. New Amsterdam in 1614, Beverswyck in 1630, Schenectady in 1662, Amsterdam in the Mohawk Valley in 1716, Utica in 1793, Lake Pleasant in 1795, Long Lake in 1830, Indian Lake in 1845—these are the dates (as nearly as I could discover) of the first houses, but it must be remembered that white men, the *coureurs de bois,* had run through every valley, that in some cases lumber had been taken, and that by 1861 the last moose had been shot out of the country.

With the vast areas of the Empire State that were more richly soiled, more readily acquirable, it is, at first, difficult to see why any white men should choose to locate within the area of the North Woods. But the blood of the frontiersmen still raced in the national veins; the freedom of untimbered reaches and the hazards of new valleys

AN ABORIGINAL APPROACH

haunted the Boones of the North. The long period between the confounding of Burgoyne and the expansions following the War of 1812 was an age of individual prowess and isolated occupation along the natural waterways of "The Dark and Bloody Ground." It was a half century of racial meetings,—and partings.

For the Indian it was a time of twilight and eclipse. The last great war parties had come from the north and been forgotten. One of them left a flotilla of a thousand canoes at the head waters of the St. Regis where they were discovered later under the mold of a century, the reminder of some massacre. Imperceptibly the dusky wanderers faded from actual encounter into hearsay, and finally into tradition. It is well for them that there was a Parkman to portray the real Iroquois whose name was his proudest boast—"The men who surpass all others."

The patroon had gone, too, with the wigwam, and babies who no longer woke crying at some shivery war-whoop were also no longer lullabied to the cradle strains of:

> "Trip a trop a troontjes,
> De varkens in de boontjes,
> De koetzes in de klaver,
> De paarden in de haver,
> De eenjes in de waterplas,
> De kalf in de lang gras,
> So groot mijn kleine poppetje was."

The "bo' jour," too, was but a broken echo from the St. Lawrence outposts, though, from the western wilderness in 1815, drifted strange reports of revelries where the brother of Napoleon had bought a hundred thousand acres in a vain effort to mingle the perfumes of Versailles with the scents of the wilderness.

Yearly the meetings of the history-makers grew less frequent and yearly the thin tide of home-makers crept up from the south. These were mainly Irish and Scotch, the inveterate colonizers.

At first the skin-hunters prospered. The Iroquois had talked of the Kohsaraga, the Beaver-Hunting Country; and because beaver were easy to capture, within a couple of decades after the Erie Canal had focussed the attention of merchants upon the north, it was Kohsaraga no more.

Then the prospectors told their tales. To this day one hears of Adirondack gold where mines can never be. But there was magnetic iron ore, in quantities that some day may pay the working, but which then served only to attract capital to erect ambitious iron works whose future was only disuse and decay.

Lumberers were better rewarded, and the easier valleys and nearer slopes were stripped of hemlock and white pine. Tanneries and sawmills were erected for temporary use, and the wanderer today often stumbles upon raspberry patches that

AN ABORIGINAL APPROACH

hide the moldering remains of shanties. In the older river towns of Hinckley, Corinth, and Forestport there are still told stories of brave exploits of the river men.

Though the kind of inhabitant had changed with the changing centuries until a *coureur-de-bois,* or a war-painted Iroquois would have been as unusual a sight as a Chinaman, until 1870 the land was the same game-filled paradise of shining lake and looming mountain as of old. Along the Atlantic seaboard cities were already congesting. People were beginning to take vacations, but they took them on porches or in picnics, or, if very venturous and rich, went to Europe. Thought of running up to the Adirondacks was only less harebrained than planning an air flight. It simply did not figure in the prospectuses of the railroads. These were beginning to enlarge their service and even to carry passengers on pleasure errands. The delight of camping was, in the common opinion, similar to the other pleasures of the field— usually left to asses.

But the ten years, beginning about 1880, saw a change. During the Civil War the Adirondack fastnesses had harbored men who had arrived by night and who did not leave any address at home— fugitives from the draft. Some stayed. Others returned (when one did not have to be furtive to be safe) to report on the excellence of a venison-

and-trout cuisine. And since a fish hook and a rifle comprised almost their sole need for a summer's outing, it was cheaper to take their families there than to pay the bills for this new fad of beach-front hotels. This was the genesis of the summer boarder.

To other and more legitimate ears, meanwhile, had come the report issued by a certain Verplanck Colvin, an enthusiastic woods-lover, who had surveyed the region in 1870 and returned his findings to the metropolitan world. Here was news worth attention. The millions of acres that every five years had been sold by the State for unpaid taxes began to be bought up by men who knew the value of green timber and the worth of falling water. Vast estates were bought outright for private preserves; still vaster areas were leased for the timber upon them and then allowed to lapse into the State's possession. It was all done quietly, and the few men who had made their homes in the Keene Valley, at Saranac, and down the Fulton Chain, who peddled their venison throughout the year and made scant money guiding the owners of the preserves dreamt not of its significance. There were not blazed trails then to every lake, and a guide who knew his business was as necessary as sugar in tea. And the guides did know their business. They knew their own native spots of land; they counseled wisely, shot well, and kept

AN ABORIGINAL APPROACH

their word. But they knew neither the power of money nor the greed for wealth. The long winter season saw them gather about stoves, tell long tales, and chew. There is one volume, at least, where such things may be read that were dreamt of only in the Adirondack woodsman's philosophy. Try "Adirondack Adventures," if you find some one to lend it to you, and see if Adirondack Murray does not conjure up for you these lean, rank-whiskered men, the stuffy cabin, and the whole wilderness howling just the other side of the thick plank door.

The long winter season was also rich harvest time for the timber thieves. Indeed, if Hough, Colvin, The Association for the Preservation of the Adirondacks, a succession of public-spirited governors, and tireless groups of incorruptible persons had not labored for a generation, there would have been no great North Woods for future Americans to enjoy. The people awoke to the fact that much land had escaped in the usual mysterious manner from the public treasury. Later, only by herculean efforts on the part of the few, was a succession of bills prevented from passing the legislature, which would have permitted companies to dam most of the valley land at public expense for private profit. Forest fires annually ruined large areas; the stretches of forested country rapidly decreasing in size pointed to the complete extermination of all game. Streams that had supplied trout for the taking were polluted by chemicals or dynamited for immediate gains. Bribery in the legislative bodies and ruthless destruction at the front combined for a final spurt of depredation. But victory came in the nick of time.

For years the State had been acquiring and holding lands, often denuded, to be sure, which lumber interests did not pay the taxes on. It was this nucleus of property that gave the idea for the Park. Curiously enough, in this way, avarice was its own undoing. In 1877, Hough laid down the project that Colvin had suggested. In 1885 the Forest Preserve was created, and the popular vote in 1894 set it aside for the use of all the people forever. So slow, however, was the progress of the march of the law against the forays of corruption, that not until 1908 did the number of enforcements of the law exceed the number of unpunished violations. Inasmuch, also, as the State owned less than half the acreage of forest and lake, and as careless and even criminal management of the rest endangered the entire holdings of the State, immediate action became necessary.

So in 1916, a proposition was brought before the voters of the State as to whether a bond issue for increasing the State holding should be authorized in the November election. By a great ma-

Photo by Warwick S. Carpenter

SOUTHWEST FROM PHARAOH MOUNTAIN

AN ABORIGINAL APPROACH 19

jority in New York City, and by a smaller majority over the State, the issue was approved, and the $7,500,000 made available will go far to intrench the interests of the State, and the East, for that matter. For the Adirondacks has become the great pleasure ground of immense numbers of vacationists. To have failed to back up the administration of the Park at this critical time in its existence, would have been a crime to the millions of workers in cities who will never be able to afford the time to go to the great breathing spaces of the West. Democracy, in ultimately recognizing what is best for itself, has again triumphed. And this time, before it was entirely too late.

If the adventures of the land itself were so crucial, the status of the land-holders was even more thrilling. For a hundred years the settlers had lived undisturbed, except by the severities of climate, the hardships of wilderness life, the drawbacks of the isolated. From 1880 to 1890 they had begun to realize that boarders had bank-accounts. They began to enlarge their inns, to estimate upon their next summer's takings. Mountain lamb was served throughout the year, and many of them had never seen a railroad, but these men of independence had grown subtly dependent upon the outside world.

Then came the first of a series of revolutions in their affairs. A railroad was pushed north from Remsen, splitting the wilderness. Huge domains beside it fell overnight into private hands, though some of the territory undoubtedly had been the State's. At one blow the Adirondackers were bereft of patronage and hunting grounds.

The patronage followed the rails. What was the use of tedious days on stages when steam would take one into the heart of the coveted shooting territory? Inn-keepers were left with nothing but empty beds, while new hotels with baths and billiard rooms shot up like geysers along the double steel line of the new enterprise. If the guests did not shoot the deer from the railroad trains, as kid-gloved adventurers shot the lions in Africa, it was because they were satiated. Fifty deer could be seen in an hour's run through the woods on an August day. It was all rare fun for everybody except the original settlers—the deer and the backwoodsmen.

But the second in the series of calamities followed hard upon the heels of the diverted boarders. Little kingdoms were cut out of the choicest deer ranges, and keepers stood on guard. Trails that for generations had been short cuts through the forest were found fenced, and the fence reinforced by a rifleman. It was the Saxon days of the New Forest over again, and the tragedy of William Rufus was reënacted in detail.

A preserve owner in the north, whether from too

AN ABORIGINAL APPROACH

much pride of estate or too little sense in its administering, was found shot in the back. The horse that was pulling him wandered into the village with a bleeding rump where the bullet still lodged. Searchers came upon the man, cold and past tale-bearing; but throughout the entire Adirondacks each owner of a preserve construed the attack as upon himself. Fear, spurred in cases by a guilty conscience, advised flight. The exodus, as will be remembered, was sudden, hasty, and complete. For years only the armed protectorate guarded the "camp"; the owner was examining art treasures in Europe.

Blame for the crisis was as usual almost equally deserved. The preserve owner, in most cases, had actually preserved the forest by financing the fight against the timber thief and the water-power scoundrel. Without his aid it is a question whether there would have remained anything but a desert for the inhabitant to roam over. On the other hand, the spirit of give and take in the mountains had been admirable. Every man's property was, to a certain extent, the next man's. Not only were mountain slopes and trout streams free for all, but in necessity, cabin and food as well. More than once I have spread my blankets on another man's bunk, cooked with his dishes, and known that, if he came suddenly upon me, I would not have to explain. As in the West, you were free to use another man's wood and food. The only unwritten stipulation was not to leave his dishes unwashed. Therefore the sudden influx of wealthy outsiders, with their haughty prohibitions and displays of unsuitable luxury, was a particularly hard pill to swallow after the privation caused by the move of the center of summer population from inns to railroad hotels.

Passion ebbed with time, however. Burnings of preserves grew less frequent. More people used the woods in summer, and prosperity came back. Such was the condition in 1910.

Then, as suddenly as its predecessors, came the third and greatest change in Adirondack affairs. The map was altered in a summer by the automobile. A mighty flood of gasoline washed out investments that had taken two decades to grow substantial. It swept comparative wealth back to the doors of the very old proprietors who had been ruined by the railroad and the preserves. Hotels, whose clients had formerly come for the summer, could now only claim them for a night. The backwoods innkeepers, whose only comforts had been bitter memories and a plug of tobacco, began to wear white collars on Sunday.

But the greatest change was in the Park itself. Good roads were laid along the main arteries and projected everywhere. Contractors were forced by public sentiment to expend more than a mere

AN ABORIGINAL APPROACH 23

fraction of the public money upon public needs. Centers of distribution for hunting parties swelled into villages; villages became towns. Saranac today is a young city. The railroads bettered their service in an effort to divert back a certain per cent. of the maddened motorists. The wilderness that had had its reticences for a thousand centuries grew spotty with vacationists.

The effect of all this on you, depends on what kind of a man you are. If you think in mass numbers, there is great satisfaction. If you do not, beside the feeling of exhilaration that development always gives, there runs a shadow of sadness that the woods, at last, have been found by the million; that the day of "old man Phelps" and his race is past. But, looking at the matter from neither extremity, there will be found comfort for both those who delight in society and for those who prefer the untenanted forest. Within the confines of the Park exist great possibilities for every temperament. Its boundaries enclose all that is scenically best of the central portion of the Adirondack region. The Park, counting public and private lands, embraces 3,313,564 acres. Forty-eight per cent. of this belongs to the State; fifteen per cent. is private preserve; six per cent. small private holdings; twenty-three per cent. belongs to lumber companies; six per cent. is improved, and the remaining two per cent. is retained by mineral companies. The recent bond issue will bring the State's holdings well over the halfway mark. In another chapter will be detailed the varied uses to which any visitor, whether New Yorker or not, may put this princely estate.

There seems but one more dimension for expansion, and that a matter of the calendar. Time was when July and August saw the season finished. Then, when some stubborn beauty lover stayed, and Labor Day ceased to tyrannize, September had a chance to exercise her charms. Husbands went up to bring their ladies home, and stayed to shoot. Now, from mid-December to March, one may wander into the woods with snow-shoes and be regarded as neither childish nor unbalanced. Indeed, some say a mid-winter night's dream is by far the fairest of all.

With this bare outline of the story of the Park, I must be content. It is only too easy to go on and on, to expand the obvious while forgetting that, of all persons who deserves the inverted thumb, he is foremost who starts out as guide and ends up with the garrulity of the seeing-everything man. One must expose the dangers; one should point out the routes that better the arrival; but not to let the traveler discover the chief glories for himself is an act that deserves shooting at sunrise. So do not expect either Luggins or my-

AN ABORIGINAL APPROACH

self to stamp, explain and vivisect the beauties of the road.

Despite all modern conveniences, the Adirondack wilderness remains. Despite the upholstered car, the thermos flask, the automatic fusillader, the mountains furnish humble pleasures that can never be exhausted. Seldom were our travels salted with superlatives. Indeed, the chief danger lay in our tendency to revel in the smallness of our pleasures. In rereading this log I find the greatest fault is just that. The data are explicit, the beauties taken for granted. You must begin, then, to wonder why Lynn and I, having seen some of the West's best wonders came to love this lake-starred, balsam forest better than that dazzling land nearer the setting sun.

CHAPTER II

NORTH CREEK TO CHIMNEY MOUNTAIN

WE set out rather self-consciously, I remember, and with an air of cavalcade. Lynn led off in knickerbockers and flannel shirt with a small pack-basket on his back. His little Western horse followed, as he had grown well accustomed to do on Wyoming trails, with the blanket rolls, the little tent, and the provisions that were meant to see us through the first stage of our independence. A soft south wind and I brought up the rear. I carried the fishing-rods, and the June sun promised an over-tardy spring at last. The red-winged blackbirds and the meadow-larks could not keep it to themselves.

To Lynn and myself about all that was of importance loomed before us; our baggage, a set of virgin mountains, and vacation. The vacation seemed capacious enough, viewed from the large end. The duffle bags did n't. They looked a trifle bulgy. So did the mountains. That was about all one could say for them when reminiscences of Montana rose to the lips only to die there out of deference to our new adventure. Indeed, I was a trifle worried at the outset because from the memories of a youthful trip I had drawn upon my comrade's credulity to the point of making a summer of it in the Adirondacks. And now the Adirondacks did not rise to the occasion.

But Lynn had set himself to outwhistling the birds, and Luggins fairly beamed at the prospect, as well he might,—a winding easy road, much grass in sight, and none of those familiar precipices with which his former excursions with us had been strewn! So, gratified, as if I were responsible for the drenching sunlight and the fresh-foliaged hills, I began to tread on air. After much packing and much planning we were off.

There was perhaps a subtler reason for the glee at our setting forth. We had had to spend the night at North Creek, and North Creek may best be described as a most excellent point to depart from. It exists chiefly for people to leave it. And doubtless it has grown so calloused to farewells that it has given over any attempts to make the departing guest sorrow at the prospect. Certainly we did n't.

If the hotels of North Creek suffer from the transitoriness of their guests, the town itself, indeed, any town, would suffer by comparison with its surroundings. On one side the stripling Hudson glitters and slides; on the other Gore Mountain's slopes and foot-hills wrinkle into alluring distances of green. And, as if for a day, the strings of houses straggle tawdrily between, advertising the drinks and tobaccos in a way to make the advertiser infamous.

Our road clung to the river for a smart hour's pacing. Only the telegraph wires were to show that the world of shopkeepers was not permanently at our backs. And on them occasionally played a tune—the wild tune that Thoreau loved most to hear. Also bluebirds, kingbirds, swallows sat upon them. And all the time the shallow, rippling Hudson, with its stranded logs, turned some corner and showed us further into the heart of the highlands.

At North River we had such a dinner as was to be remembered, country style and country courtesy and all five courses for fifty cents. Luggins, too, made industrious use of the occasion and showed a sorry reluctance to resume the road for one who had been fattened for a pilgrimage. But one o'clock saw us turning to the southwest and away from the river, with constantly rising spirits. That very night was to bed us under stars.

As we were much surprised to find, our mode of travel appeared to throw nearly every one into a fever of curiosity or concern. In the West not an eyebrow would have been raised if we had started to cross the Staked Plains with the same outfit, but in North Creek we had noticed no metropolitan reticence concerning our peculiarity, and at the little hotel where we lunched some guides predicted misadventure ahead. We gathered that to go conventionally in the Adirondacks one must travel either by stage, in a motor bus or private automobile, on foot or in canoes.

But we had faith in Luggins. He was a birthright member in the pragmatic school of optimists. Like *God* in Browning's mad poem, he never said a word, even at murder. There was no vicissitude that he had not gone through. His ordinary course was unpretentious plodding, but he would have scaled the Alps if we had led him on. He was willing at any moment to sleep or swim, fast or feast, as necessity demanded. And we grew to have an exaggerated tenderness for the crooked streak of white down his nose.

By the turn of the afternoon we had left the highway and plunged down steeply for a few rods through the woods to come upon the lake called Thirteenth Lake, a continuation, I suppose, of the Fulton Chain that runs bravely up to Eighth and stops perplexed like the *Parson* in the "One Hoss Shay."

Thirteenth Lake runs southwest by northeast as do nearly all the Adirondack waters. The shadow was just commencing to steal out from the lee of the mountain on its farther shore, half a mile away, when we stopped on the little promontory that had apparently been created for our camp site. It took but a moment to dispossess Luggins of his load and but another to arrange our apartment. At the risk of seeming to gloat, I am intruding the details, just this once.

Lynn and I had been pals on so many of these parties that we worked with the silence and precision of knitting needles. Our foremost discovery had been that two can accomplish more upon one job by coöperation that they can by dividing the chores into each-man-for-himself operations. We both put up the tent, both chopped the firewood, both cooked, and both ate.

Probably during the progress of this account there will intrude an itemized list of household gods. It is a temptation too traditional to be eluded. Where is the camper who writes or the writer who camps who has ever let slip the chance to corrupt some other's comfort with his own contraptions? The delight to preach is too universal whether it be in a promulgation of the pulpit or in an exhortation on some fantastic frying-pan.

But not now is the time to gloat upon our contentments. Now but two articles demand description—our tent and our beds. The tent was a baker of brown waterproofing. A baker tent is the sort that opens to the fire along the entire front and entails unnecessary labor for quite unnecessary comfort. For a one-night stand it can be set up in a few minutes; for an indefinite stay it can be made elaborately cheerful. At any time it affords the luxuries of dryness, warmth, and space in which to have one's being. The amount of wood that can be burned before a baker through an autumn night is more than a matter of sentiment. It means hard labor—indeed, the unnecessary labor to which I referred, for other tents will do. But so will your town house, if it comes to a question of being easy. Lynn and I would have put up our baker at any cost just for the unindustrious hour of after-supper. To loaf before the great backlog, with the forest freshness drifting in at the sides, and your spirits soaring under the quite inadequate heavens, is the best privilege of a hard day.

Bed comes next. Our beds had been the text of many a speculation and experiment during our past trips. We had foreborne to request Luggins to carry cots, and yet we refused to sleep on bare ground or balsam tips plucked at a too large cost of time. Air cushions were too expensive and sleeping bags too warm. Our solution was the cot, after all, but minus its woodwork. With the canvas hooked upon two parallel logs, securely staked apart, each could procure him the easiest and most somnifacient bed in the world for the carriage of two pounds of canvas and the necessary quilts and blankets to keep him warm. And these we wished upon Luggins without qualm.

How much humanity there is in the act of pitching a tent! The race seems more tender in the deed. It compounds all the past and sweetest emotions—door-stone, hearthstone, shelter, home. They are all there, renewed each setting-up time with a newness that house-buying never feels. But with Lynn and myself the rite began always with a bit of folly that I find we share with most pitchers of tents. We always had an eye to the view. The practice was even more preposterous than the theory.

The theory presupposed that we would retire at sunset with the glorious orb fading away behind the encrimsoned peaks, that we would drowse off with the evening star etching itself into our dreams, and that we would awake to the enjoyment of limpid beams upspringing from a gilded horizon. The theory is flattery. The reality is disillusion. We mostly turned in dog-tired and rather late. We fell asleep with the usual speed of falling bodies. We woke in the extremity of hunger. We rose with never a glance at the horizon. There was no margin for rhapsody and only a legendary interest in anything but breakfast. And yet we always posed that tent. I trust that a subtler influence than logic can suspect, ratified the instinct.

Making all allowances for first enthusiasms,

TO CHIMNEY MOUNTAIN

Thirteenth Lake retains a comeliness in our memories that more gifted localities do not. It composed, as we found, all the essentials of an excellent base for beginnings into a tract of interest and beauty. Its woods were wild but not remote; its climbs steep, but not drastic. Its fish catchable.

The next morning turned bracing cool before a west wind. Great white clouds put on sail in a sky that shone blue and spacious. And we set forth to overlook the country from a small mountain called Peaked. The excursion developed into an engaging little climb. In a boat, which we borrowed from a genial gentleman in overalls, we crossed the lake. A trail followed a tiny stream to its source in Peaked Mountain Pond, and turned to the right. The last few yards of the ascent was almost mountaineering, being bare and rugged rock. From the summit there opened out a view that is not too common from the lower Adirondack peaks, which, under altitudes of thirty-five hundred feet, are usually wooded. In the direction of the Hudson River stretched the green and white checkerboard of settlement and clearing, while on the other sides rolled the almost unbroken forest. Above us the summery clouds promised a truce between storms for several days. Though rising only a few hundred feet, Peaked was a most satisfying mountain.

We entertained our boat-lender at a luncheon. Lynn contributed corn-bread, and I, sunnies, caught at the overalled gentleman's advice. He had said: "If you row up to the inlet yonder, you'll have some real smart fishin'. You kin catch all you kin eat at twenty throws." And I had. Fat sunnies fried in butter shall not masquerade as bass, nor yet as trout, but men back from climbing do not eat them listlessly for all that.

Our guest, who, in his duller moments pursued a trade at North Creek, spent much of his time, he told us, at Thirteenth Lake. Between applications of corn-bread and maple syrup the good man vouchsafed us much first-hand information on the neighborhood. He told us that we would see many deer at Hour Pond, a circular shallow of picturesque water where lily pads grow extravagantly. He held us by accounts of the wilderness about Botheration Flow. He talked of the garnet mines in the vicinity. And we went with him to his little shack to see a large stone that he had found.

Our eyes were mostly for the shack; it was such an example of slovenliness. Newspapers of historic times, clothes of the same date, ingredients of past and future meals, bedclothes, were all part of the baggage of this unspeakable den. How a gentleman who had escaped from North Creek to

Photo by Warwick S. Carpenter

FOREST COVER: BRANT LAKE COUNTRY

TO CHIMNEY MOUNTAIN 37

the woods could fraternize with such filth in the respectable society of forest trees and beside the clean waters is a mystery that laziness alone does not explain. Occasionally among the Adirondack hermits you will find one, slothful and revolting when it comes to sanitation and the broom, though otherwise full of good sense. But for the most part the trappers, the woodsmen, and guides, who spend much of their time alone, are excellent housekeepers. Their dishes are always washed, their wood-bins filled, their clothes sewed with the carefulness of sailors. It is oftener the people of cities who live catch as catch can.

We were in a hurry to reach the Kunjamuk country and on that account neglected to profit by the old man's cheerful descriptions of many places. But we did go up Gore Mountain. It attains the respectable altitude of 3540 feet and gives one a look-off into blue counties. The view was not so interesting, barring the charming prospect of the Hudson's valley, as the descent on the western side. There is unfrequented wildland, indeed. You sink into thick mosses, at peril to your legs. You climb great fallen trunks. It is just the sort of wet and secretive wilderness that neither repels by inaccessibility nor attracts by special beauty. You would expect the warblers to nest there in content. From our night encampment along Botheration Flow we heard the first barred owl barking; leagues off it seemed, across the wide and lonely wilderness.

Botheration Flow, like King's Flow and the other flows, is a watercourse of special design, peculiarly misnamed. There is no flow. The natural ambition of a stream is to get somewhere. But a flow, having been thwarted by reduced valley slope or beaver dams or human agency, barely creeps. The result is excellent canoeing. On these flows it is possible to paddle for miles, or to fish from a boat where spring holes harbor trout, to surprise deer at nightfall, or simply float on an inverted sky in the amazing twilight beauty of these water-lanes. They are numerous in all parts of the Park except the northeastern. And Botheration, which was our first, grappled us to it with speedy attachment. We finally returned our borrowed canoe to our dirty counsellor with a regret that was only surpassed by our desires to be forwarded upon our journey. Beautiful as the Thirteenth region was, it was but the threshold of the woods, and the unbroken forest ahead made us uneasy with its call. Before we went, however, we obtained permission from the owner to overhaul his haggard den. It was a ghoulish job, but we felt distinctly better for having repaid him for his loans by the sweat of a profound housecleaning.

In the secluding mists of early morning we set

Luggins again to his interrupted profession. Our winding road took us in the general direction of Indian Lake. The tops of the moderate mountains that lay beside us were not visible, but alternate openings and meetings of the wood offered the variety that devours the miles. There was a vague loneliness of the landscape caused by uninhabited clearings. It was superior in degree to the aloofness of the forest itself. The prepared spaces seemed to long for an occupancy and a business of which the uncleared land did not hint. Lynn and I both felt this, and after the day's march, when we pitched our tent by a meadow, rank with uncut hay, the domestic wildness lay upon our spirits. We were glad to make an early night of it.

In the morning lifted clouds showed what a superb sleeping room we had unwittingly found. Our one object had been to gratify Luggins' deep desire for the rich meadow-grass. Our own breakfast was eaten before a landscape of subdued beauty. Toward the west flanking hills dipped sharply and through the wide vale rose Snowy Mountain, master by a head of his long range. This side of him lay Indian Lake, invisible. Below us shone a bright arc of the King's Flow. To the south the valley of the dark Kunjamuk invited, while behind us rolled the green shoulders of mountains.

THE ADIRONDACKS

Late May and June are the great bird months of the Adirondacks. However still the woods may be at other seasons of the year, in the mating month there is too much joy to be swallowed up by the grim spruces. Clearings become orchestral, and even the deep forest has its songs. Whoever has heard the whitethroat in some remote valley or the hermit thrush from the deep wood at evening has been bound with invisible strings to the wilderness. The long sweet warbling of a flock of purple finches is tenderness itself.

By July there are gaps in the chorus, and soon after an infinite quiet settles upon the forest, broken by sounds that only he that hath ears to hear will have the sensibility to detect.

The immediate goal of campers by King's Flow is a curious formation called Chimney Mountain which does everything a chimney should do, but smoke. This unique structure, lying about seven miles to the southeast of Indian Lake Village, rises in a sixty-foot pinnacle from a mountain already 2650 feet in the air. Mr. William J. Miller in a New York State Museum Bulletin explains the interesting geologic formation by erosion. He states that an inclined plane of rock weathered on the under side of its upper end until a huge block cracked off. This left the tower and a rift, 650 feet long, 250 deep, and 300 wide, with a slope at an angle of fifty degrees. The appearance of the crater-like cavity beside the chimney is misleading, and visitors are inclined to defraud erosion of its due by ascribing the fissures, pinnacle, and crater to volcanic action. Although it is not, the spectacle is unique in the Adirondacks, and we found it and the view worth the clamber.

And, in the name of all that is rude, that was an aggravating ascent! For, after ten minutes over fields and ten through open wood by a pellucid brook, we came to one of those arrangements of the devil, known as a burn. On this side of the mountain, the west, the rise is nearly a thousand feet in half a mile, and that is pretty stiff going. The burn made it seem like ten thousand, for a burn is nature's barbed-wire entanglement. The fire had burned off the wood loam, and a million rocks projected. The sound-looking places let us through. Fallen trees criss-crossed at the height of our waists, too sticky to crawl under, too hard to flounder over. We had to wiggle through. In the less cumbered spots, briers bloomed to heaven. The sun came out with violence. We were thirty minutes crossing this fallacious short-cut which an able kangaroo could have done in twenty leaps. Weeks later we learned that there is a long way round by a trail—and probably a still longer hunt for it.

By a series of disablements we at last emerged from the narrow zone at the entrance to a cave, which, unlike the Sibyl's, spouted not hot air, but cool. It was a fissure in the wall of the mountain, with a small opening at the top. This broadened as it descended. We let down our sweating selves between its dripping walls with gratitude. In the interior dimness we crawled upon snow covered with dirt and small stones. Later, when we came to inquire about this singular mountain which had a refrigerator as well as a chimney, we learned that on ordinary summers the supply of snow lasted into the autumn, sometimes the season round.

Lynn, of course, coveted a seat upon the unsteady-looking chimney. I reminded him of the half-gale that was now blowing from the northwest, and of his home and mother. There seemed to be little actual danger. Indeed when he waved to me, I began to follow and, once starting, disliked to stop. I huddled close to the rocks, inserting my fingers in the crevices. The wind piped at my ears. In fact at the time there seemed no reason why a harder puff should not waft me off and down to the gravestones below.

But from the pinnacle much of the amiable provinces of Warren and Hamilton Counties spread before us. On the north lay an open valley, with the clay-colored road slashing here and there into a hill. It was the State road that runs from North Creek to Indian Lake Village. To the

TO CHIMNEY MOUNTAIN 43

west and south rose the mountains about Indian Lake. Bellying clouds threw a wash of shadow over the forest and clearings. And always did old Kunjamuk draw attention to his post in the south. I have seen this mountain from every side and in every weather, but never, even at the sunniest does he lose his aspect of piratical blackness.

The wind howled cheerfully at our turret, and my distrust of the descent was only exceeded by my definite dislike for freezing on the Chimney. Yet going down was not so bad as I expected. Only once did I have to cling to the ledge while my feet groped for their inch of standing room. But I do remember thinking that if my remains were to garnish the bottom of some precipice I hoped it would be a taller one—the Jungfrau's, perhaps, or the Grand Canyon.

We got back to our tent in time to catch some trout from King's Flow for lunch, and since Luggins was still stowing ballast considerably to hayward, we went into consultation with the map.

There are, in the main, but two varieties of travelers—the tourist and the tramp.

The tourist leaves nothing to chance or to the gods. He knows weeks ahead just where he is to stop and how much he is going to tip the waiter. A time-table stimulates him like strong drink. He intoxicates himself with railway folders, and the more complicated the routing, the better he is pleased. Such creatures enjoy the things they see, I am forced to suppose, but I wager it is only if the sights do not conflict with the guide-book.

The tramp, on the other hand, is touchy about plans. For him the worst thing that can be said about a trip is that it was premeditated. For him the first fine cream of the road must not be skimmed by the descriptions of any guide. He must have no times definitely scheduled, no spaces exactly measured out. Such creatures eat, I presume, but it must be done extemporaneously.

Lynn's temperament and mine fell well within these lines. We often differed and sometimes disagreed, fortunately, for by complaisance fell the angels. But both of us were content, after the skeleton of our adventures was arranged, to let the complexion of the moment be decided by the moment. Our scheme was for each to state his desire as plausibly as he could and then we would bide by the golden mean. This had worked so well on our other trips that we had long ago lost any false unselfishness in the preliminary statement of ambitions. In our compromises we would have made Henry Clay blush like a dilettante.

In this case our question was three-fold; whether to strike across through three hours of woodland to the shores of Indian Lake where friends of ours were encamped, or to take a day's circuit by Indian Lake Village and thence to their camp, or to spend a week in the march around to Speculator. The decision was not difficult, this time, for in the backs of our two heads was beginning to blossom the scheme of seeing the Adirondack Park from top to bottom, and from side to side. If Lynn can claim any of the more forbidding virtues, it is that of thoroughness. Later I found out that he secretly intended to see every mile of our highland wilderness, and I had secretly already begun to take notes. So the zealot in both of us voted for the long detour. In twenty minutes we had reaped a bundle of hay for Luggins' breakfast and in twenty more were nosing our way south over the dilapidations of an old logging road.

CHAPTER III

WE TRAVEL NORTH BY SOUTH

ALTHOUGH we were only a short distance out from North Creek, yet the routine of our travel was already set. Luggins understood that he was to demand drink of the frequent streamlets not more than once an hour. Lynn and I each carried a light pack basket for the chinaware and the extras. Luggins probably wished that we would carry more.

When in the mood, we talked of all things under heaven and a few above it. But as often as not we would be silent for a league of woodland, the rhythm of the marching being sufficiently potent for one's dreams. We got along, as they say, beautifully. A sense that certain bounds of politeness must never be overstepped contributed. Also, life was so full of a number of things that we never felt circumscribed. There must have been crises, but we swallowed them, silent. And we never approached that *impasse* of pertinacity that breaks the relations of trappers or prospectors in greater solitudes for longer periods. Close travel for many weeks demands a fraternity that is too intimate to be lightly entered upon. Yet to find a comrade for the long hike is worth many an experiment on shorter tours. The full savor of wild life can come only to those most happily bonded for their work in sun and rain.

That night we camped by a little brook, called Silver on the map. It was a refreshing spot, though it would have been hideously lonely for just one person. It had been a lonely sort of day —a day shut in by forests of spruce and sugar-maple, birch and balsam. We had only the most occasional glimpses of the by-lying territory. We had journeyed, to be sure, upon a man-made road, but mosses softened the ancient ruts, and there was nothing else to show that human beings traversed the country twice a year. As we sat about our early supper not even a chipmunk infringed upon the stillness. The dimness dripped with the primeval. The occasion belonged clearly to the dryads. Tired with the long tramp, we let their solemnities seal the day for us in sleep.

The next morning, after much refreshment, an ill-starred glance at the map suggested that we ascend nearby Dug Mountain for the outlook it would give us upon our neighbors. Leaving Luggins trying to conceal his satisfaction, we followed the thread of Silver to a deserted lumber camp. For half an hour we mounted a ridge, bore to the left, toiled under a feverish sun toward the elusive summit. With each step upward we streamed more incontinently. When is a windfall not a windfall? When it's in your way. A broad burn and the incline made progress an exacting torment. Gravity and good sense bade us turn about. But, though it probably is a sign of unsound intellect, Lynn refused to be interviewed about reconsidering the ascent. So after another brutal quarter of an hour we stood upon what may have been the summit. Although the eminence rises to upwards of three thousand feet we still had to climb a tree to get a view.

The view was swathed in heat. Filling the whole west, stretched Indian Lake, slender and shining under the Snowy Range. At the south gleamed Whittaker, and immediately below were three gemlets, called the Dug Mountain Ponds. We returned to Luggins by way of them. I believe that they are being lumbered now. On one there was a grove of white pines rising into blue-green heights greater than I have seen elsewhere in the Park. Under them we gratefully ate a little lunch. We lay on the soft needles, listening to the soft stir of the wind and resting. It was a spot for tired bodies to soak up comfort, and for taut spirits to bathe in the securities of peace.

Late in the afternoon, indeed so late that a round moon was rising over a round mountain, we entered Speculator. It is a comfortable place

WE TRAVEL NORTH BY SOUTH 49

with white-painted houses and a long white inn, clamorous with children and their nurses. The village sits a little back from Lake Pleasant to have a view of Speculator Mountain, and, barring the children, seems void of animation. It is a day's stage from the railroad, old style, and at the very end of its street, as we found in conversation with the post-office, begins a hinterland of trout and bear.

But Speculator, despite the trout and the bear, presents itself to my memory as the paradise for children as our adventure with its lake attests. We had followed the street to the water's edge and then went along the water's edge for half a mile in order to screen the village from our view. On such a night we scorned hotel rooms and yet we were weary from the Dug Mountain climb of the morning. So we took few pains with our beds, fatally few. The full moon was caught by the lake in plains of glory. The noises from the village hushed one by one. Perfect night was about us, and the hills grew ghostly with moonshine. But I was too tired. The occasional wakefulness that assails one every so often in the woods struck home. I lay there in luxuries of light, but with barely a wink of sleep. The trip of the mornning seemed as part of a past lifetime. I began to look forward to the morning plunge.

But in this lake designed for children it was

not to be. The water was insufferably shallow. The lake had a magnificent sand bottom, just the thing for wading, but the bottom had very little lake. We waded out and waded out. Yet it was only about one foot deep. Another hundred yards and Lynn sat down in desperation and began to pour the lake over him. Through the cold mists of dawn shapely mountains rose from the distant shores. To a person not affected with a zeal for diving it was a kindly scene. To us it was disappointing: delightful, horizontally, but vertically, childish.

Although **Lake Pleasant** and Sacandaga, its twin, are surrounded by private holdings, there is much State land to the west and south for camping and hunting. The elevations are not high, but the situations are charming, and the wilderness in which the Canada creeks take their rise is a wilderness indeed. There are no roads, no villages. Here and there is a sequestered shack built by the guides for the hunting season. In addition, there is something to hunt.

For sheer joy in comfortable exploration one can stumble upon no more appetizing country than the richly wooded, high-shouldered, and well-watered slopes to the west of Piseco Lake. From an inciting eminence we looked upon these fields, so Elysian for wayfarers; but as we were to make our incursions from another sallying-point, we

WE TRAVEL NORTH BY SOUTH 51

desisted. We turned our backs upon Piseco, retraced our steps to Speculator, replenished our stores for a future of unknown duration at a neat corner emporium, and quit the district by a long and upright road.

The incline of the hill devoured the breath. But at the top we hovered a moment over as cheering a panorama of cultivation and green fields as any man with a little farmer in the blood might travel fifty miles to see. Yet it held us only for a moment. The fresh and unknown wilderness lay before, and we gladly turned our backs upon the village with its church and fields.

From sunny farm-house to unpainted shack, from shack to uninhabited clearing, from clearing to unfrequented wood, the road bore us, and the radiant morning permitted no sluggishness in thought or gait. It was difficult not to run and sing. Only the desire not to appear too ridiculous in Luggins' eyes prevented us.

It was not going so well with all the world, however. Around a turn we came upon a Ford, stalled mid-hill, with three men in mackinaws in session about it. They looked upon our cavalcade with envy, I thought. Luggins was at least moving. A young Scandinavian was experimenting under the hood, and the two old Irishmen, gray of hair and quizzical of countenance, were engaged in thought. Machinery out of order was as much of a temptation to Lynn as an Irishman was to me; so we stopped.

They were in luck, for I wager there was nobody within the Park so good at an amateur autopsy as my companion. Unlike myself! I appreciate motoring. It is a gift of the gods like maple syrup and the new moon, something to be enjoyed as long as possible. But if it resolves itself into an argument of cylinders and mixtures, I am willing to have the bill sent in. I suspect, at times, that Lynn wants the things to give out just to enjoy the pleasures of resuscitation. I am only grateful that he takes Luggins for granted without a dissection. Perhaps it is because he is only one cylinder.

Lynn's masterly motions and profound enjoyment awed the men in mackinaws. They regarded him with deference, and when he coaxed the first plaintive cadences and finally a continuous purr from the stalled brute, a relieved conversation broke out. They told us that they had been working all winter on a large lumbering operation on Whittaker Lake. Large areas awaited cutting. We confided our route to them. They proposed a detour to their camp which promised interest. Then the Scandinavian took the wheel, and with a parting convulsion, they left us. Lynn looked after the clattering car until it had topped the rise, and for an instant I thought I detected long-

North From Pharaoh Mountain

Photo by Warwick S. Carpenter

ing in his gaze. But I did him an injustice. He set out after Luggins and me with his old appetite for the road undiminished, and when he caught up with us, he said a little wistfully:

"Do you suppose they are all like that? A lumber camp can't be any more romantic than a ranch."

Even so. The men of a lumber camp are mostly middle-aged and always tired. Their hours are long; they eat in silence, smoke in silence, sleep. If there ever was romance about their life, it has vanished. Wherever there is humanity, there is a story, but the cattle raiser and the wood-chopper of to-day bury it beneath slovenly surfaces. Yet there are camps in the Adirondacks, which we fell upon later, that proved cleanly as well as hospitable, ambitious as well as hard-working. Generalizations are not generous.

We turned Luggins from his road of ease to follow the telephone wire as by direction. It led us through caverns of green giant beeches, with pyramids of the most succulent green boughs for their roofs. There were ancient pines that had been proud treelings when Henry Hudson was learning Dutch. Swarthy spruces and magnificent sugar-maples walled in the luxurious maze of our advance. Languid sunlight fell in places, but an eerie gloom increased. But the weather outside was distant as if outside a house.

After an hour through the somber forest, out we came upon some buildings beside a gray lake. The sky was filmed, the glorious blue of the morning but a memory. In Wyoming we had never needed a tent in summer. In the Adirondacks no morning sky could foretell the evening. The weather was either a dazzling uncertainty or a drizzling certainty. Within fifteen minutes after our arrival upon Whittaker the mist curtain had descended upon the great, wooded shoulders of Dug Mountain. At the lumber house we were welcomed by the "missus." She was much too thin and pale-eyed for a dweller in the palace of health. But the impending storm rather than her lean and hungry look decided us to hasten. We exaggerated about the size of our last meal, telephoned to Master Thomas, the friend whose camp we were aiming for, across the miles of wilderness, and were again engulfed in the afternoon shadows of the wood.

For the first time on our trip all was not plain sailing. Master Thomas had explained our route with the neat science of a woods-traveler. He had told us to skirt Whittaker, follow a trail to the Jessup River, proceed down the right bank to the entrance of Dug Mountain Brook, and wait there until he appeared with the launch. But the trail had been much defaced by lumbering operations; the sky was a seamless and dripping drab; our spirits had lost the impetus of breakfast and not yet felt the spur of an anticipated supper. We began to think of our despised lumber lunch with tenderness.

Though hungry, we were not yet entirely insensible to the majestic woods. A fine rain had begun to fall. We heard it pattering upon the green roof, but we walked dry in somber cloisters as if in a different world. At length we came out into a natural clearing, very much like the wild meadows of the West, and doubtless beautiful to persons in a dry and well-fed condition. But to us it was a desert island. The trail led in, but none led out. Encumbered with Luggins, we dared not contemplate striking through to the Jessup by compass. We were marooned, and if in no danger of dying of thirst, we were in some peril of the opposite. Lynn remarked that he was going to restore the balance of power by getting some of the water inside him. So we set about making ourselves some tea while Luggins ate the juicy grass. It was as curious a party as I remember.

Master Thomas appeared just as we were done. If I had been concocting this narrative, I could not have arranged his entrance more dramatically. To a stranger he was a quick, short, grizzled man, whose observations were interesting. To Lynn and me he had been an open-air comrade, a keen-sighted counselor. Years before at school he had taught us algebra and animals, logarithms and love of the woods. Now, although his sons were older than we, he was still to be counted upon to furnish an active sympathy for our exploits.

His first remark was typical. Instead of asking us why we were having afternoon tea by a drenched meadow like two Mad Hatters, he praised us for letting ourselves be so easily found. In a moment he had won Luggins for life by letting him nose a piece of maple sugar out of his coat pocket. Talking industriously about the trout fishing that he was going to show us, he led the way at a brisk pace to the dianesque cove wherein Dug Mountain Brook merged forever with the broadening Jessup. The motor-boat lay in wait, and Luggins justified our boast of his being the most versatile and best self-adjusting creature in existence by consenting to stand on the bottom.

Indian Lake is a ribbon of water nine miles long and about a mile wide. At its upper end it divides. One three-mile branch lies in the Jessup River valley which was submerged when the dam was made. Above the slack water the little stream sparkles through woods to which the beaver have come back. Opposite the Dug Mountain Brook outlet lies a trail which takes one over to Mason Lake and the Miami River, a marvelous home of trout and beaver. If you follow the

Miami's aldered curvings, you are at last entranced by the Sabbath beauties of Lewey Lake. It lies under the Snowy Range, sandy-beached and forest-shored. It empties into Indian's other arm, and if you paddle around the long point and up through the beautiful rocky passage crowned with beeches, you will find the sequestered camp called Back Log. Thither our conglomerate launch load was tending. You will have to screen for yourself the drama of our reception: two wanderers, tired and wet and hungry, a patient packhorse, some hospitable hand-shakings, a tent to dress in before which a full-tongued fire licked at a giant birch-log, premonitions of an imminent meal in the air. Camping has two rewards, nay, three: the anticipation, the time being, and the afterward.

Indian Lake makes as fine a forest headquarters as the Adirondacks afford. Wooded shores rise on all sides, and to the north on the fairest days the Marcy Mountains show blue. Snowy, with its attendants, fairly gluts the west, and Kunjamuk lords it in melancholy to the east. At the northern end of the lake a small cottage colony has built; the remainder of the hundred miles of shore line is State land. Unfortunately the water is partly drawn off on dry seasons, leaving an unsightly residuum of logs and stumps. But there is always enough liquid left to float the enormous pickerel. Elijah would never have needed to call in the ravens if he had struck Indian Lake with a pickerel spoon. The in-flowing streams are scatteringly inhabited by trout. It is a hospitable wilderness. Little ponds lie back from the big lake. And some of these, Crotched and Johnny Mack and Round, left in our memories some intimate scenes to be cherished.

It began to rain, at first steadily from the east, and then impartially from every part of the compass. And then we were vouchsafed a morning of crystal and blue that shouted, "Snowy!" in our ears.

I shall be all my life deciding, I suppose, whether it be better to hustle about the world and see the sights, with a sort of understanding, of course; or to master the ravines and hillocks of one domestic neighborhood; whether it be nearer living to worship before Fuji-yama and the Matterhorn or to know well the intricacies and secrets of a single vale. It is a rending decision. Will you have star-spaces or flowers in the crannied wall?

Snowy is the sort of mountain that is negligible in size, when compared with your Mt. McKinleys—negligible, that is, except to the one carrying bed and lodging up him. He is commonplace for looks, compared with the Gothic splendors of the Alps. He fronts you with a bold precipice or two. He

WE TRAVEL NORTH BY SOUTH 61

rises out of decent woods. He scorns to lure with any waterfall of particulars. Yet Snowy has his moods, his beauties, his sternnesses, and the hearts of those who know him.

We set out, Master Thomas leading. For thirty minutes the trail kept a decent sense of direction under great trees, and then took to the brook. Up the brook we scrabbled on inclined slabs of mother rock till a wall, a few hundred feet high, sets one to the right. Another half hour, sufficiently upright to borrow all one's wind, and there was the fire warden's cabin. A little turn and we were out on top.

To scale Gibraltar is a matter you would never heed with Master Thomas guiding. He takes you on with a short step. Under his shrewd brow shine shrewd eyes that miss nothing of the contour of the country. It is he that points out our first fawn. It is he that finds the rare flower. Evening camps with him are a feast of woodlore and a flow of soul as well. The sharpness in those eyes is mainly humor and twinkle. For resource and wisdom he is the wiry woodmaster of us all.

We found the fire warden seizing the fair day to mend his housekeeping. Can hermits think? Or have they just the two gratifications: reading last month's magazine and not being struck by lightning? This man, spare and forty-five, whose muscles had been hardened by the log-drive and who was taking the rest cure—was he becoming just another part of the azure, drenched wonderland about him? Or did the gales that fell upon his cabin drive him to deep thought? Does the crawling stuffiness of the office-holder or the wideness of blown horizons conjure the greater vision of the universe? It is impossible to divine directly, and I am afraid my warden would not have told me no matter how obliquely I had pressed the question.

From the summit of Snowy an amazing expanse of forest-land falls away. Only to the east is much water seen. There the whole length of Indian lies white at one's feet. In the distance a few ponds glimmer, but only as foam laces wide-rolling combers. You breathe in relief to realize that, despite fire and pillage, there are such stretches of forest left.

In every view that is to refresh the memory there must remain one chief delight. And from Snowy it is not the tumble of green rollers, not even the timber blanket that I would climb to see most of all. There is a little ledge on the western side from which the slope swoops down into a perfect amphitheater. The soaring sides sink evenly to rest. From the ledge the arms of mountains appear to enclose it. Storms cannot harry it. The sun nestles into it. Quiet, driven from everywhere else, may sleep there. Even the frost leaves it for its last and most enchanting prey.

Long did we lie on the moss of the ledge, steeping in the sunshine, and the calm of the marvelous bowl below. It was a vision of serenity worth far greater struggle to attain. We forgot, for the moment, that we were on a planet that was mad.

CHAPTER IV

THE CEDAR RIVER COUNTRY

THERE is no mortal doubt that a fisherman will sacrifice himself and everybody else for his fish. Ask a fisherman what epitaph to write for him, and even if he has been a grand duke or a bard, I will wager my new rod that he would secretly prefer to have "Good Fisherman" carved upon the final stone.

Consequently, when Master Thomas looked down into the wooded country west of Snowy and traced the number of virgin streams upon the map, it was quickly decided that we would make a sortie upon the trout. The calendar was to be thrown to the winds; enough food was to be lashed upon Luggins to ameliorate any hard luck. Like Moses, we descended from the mountain with a glowing countenance.

There were two avenues of attack from our base at Back Log. Lynn and Master Thomas were to go around by Indian Lake Village with Luggins and come in by the Cedar River to a junction of three streams on the Little Moose River. That was a two days' trip. Thornton,

THE CEDAR RIVER COUNTRY 65

Master Thomas' son, and I were to take the tent, cross the range, and have camp ready. Everybody was suited.

Thornton is a man of muscle, with a mind of parts. It is a good combination for wood travel. We set out under the shining skies at dawn with gaiety. He carried the tent, a blanket, axes; I bore the food for three meals, a blanket, and the fishing rods. He had the weight, I the vexation. One cannot walk too carefully with rods.

The day warmed to our efforts. We spent much time looking for the blazes that should lead us to Squaw Brook. To add to the humor of the trip tall nettles stung us with animation. We further strained our habit of politeness by momently increasing the distance from breakfast. But by noon we had reached the Squaw, a cheerful brook on the farther side of Snowy, and within a flick of a fly some trout were sizzling in the pan. Thus does barbarism uphold convention by fortifying the amenities by a square meal.

It was well that we began that afternoon with confidence, for before sundown we were to endure every annoyance of the inhabitable wilderness short of breaking our necks.

The series began promptly with a corduroy road. Forswear such. A corduroy road is a succession of slippery tree trunks laid side by side to complicate walking over places already naturally impassable. It undoubtedly does prevent the teams of lumbermen from sinking out of sight in the mire, and in certain stages of time and tide a corduroy is an aid. But this one down the Squaw had been laid in legendary times. The logs were rotted to a degree that made each step a surmise. And if the surmise proved incorrect, you broke your leg. Above, raspberry bushes of unheard of virility entwined in handsome profusion. Decomposed bridges aggravated the crossings of the stream. And the monotony of our progress was playfully diversified by the surmounting of fallen trees at intervals. There was three miles of this.

We were now in the heart of the wilderness. Hard wood and soft wood rose in a magnificent forest which was intermingled with little undergrowth except upon our road. Twice we passed great beaver dams. From one Master Thomas had once taken thirty legal trout, stopping only because he had enough. But we resisted that temptation.

We found the Cedar River basking in the golden sunlight of mid-afternoon and the spot recommended itself for rest. The shallow stream ran between grassy banks from which the serried spruces had retreated a few rods. A delicious breeze blew down from the open sky. But I discovered that I had left my ax half a mile back at the last crossing, which had been particularly complicated. So while Thornton rested, I retraced my leaps over the corduroy. This only tended to emphasize my previous impressions of it.

But in the woods aggravations are only skin-deep. Fatigue passes soon while the beauty is eternal. As we pushed deeper and deeper into the uninhabited, past trials grew vague in the green oblivion, and our conversation again took on the detached manners of the content.

So, I suppose, it was really due to the discussion of Hindenburg's ethics or some such sublimated topic that we missed the trail. All I know is that we had gone on much longer than we ought and that my pack was asserting its existence when we discovered that it was only a deer trail that we were following. In the fading day the woods were doubtless more beautiful than ever. But it was a beauty unidentified with either food or shelter. We ignored it.

Of course we weren't lost. We were merely where we shouldn't have been, without knowing where that was. We sat down on a log to lay plans and to rest the gnats which had been over-exerting themselves to keep up. Curiously enough the stimulus of being play-lost had banished my fatigue. I was good for twenty miles, now, bar corduroy. Prudence signaled retreat, but we knew what was behind; we did not know what lay before. The sun was presumably still making for the west, although the indications made it out northeast.

Blessed are the docile for they do not get lost. It is only the stubborn who try to buck the compass. We couldn't understand why the sun should want to set in the northeast after all these years of the other thing, but as we still enjoyed the use of our intelligences we set out after him. And this proves that we weren't lost. The sun might set in the zenith without disturbing a lost man or making him pause.

Twilight was encroaching. Nevertheless, we decided to go on for half an hour before looking for a camp-site. Within five minutes we had experienced all the sensations of Balboa on his peak in Darien, for at the foot of a slope twinkled the waters of a lovely lake, and at its farther end stood a cabin from which rose the blue smoke of a new wood fire. Doubtless the cabin was lost, too, for by our map it clearly should not have been there. But we were in a condition to accept it and no questions asked.

But how to reach it awaited solution. To our right a promontory promised hard walking. To our left a stream had to be forded. We chose a wetting rather than more promenade.

The stream was deeper than we judged, thanks

THE CEDAR RIVER COUNTRY 69

to the indiscriminate industries of some beaver. The beaver is the self-made man of the forest and, I suppose, is held up to the children of the forest as such. But it is a dangerous example.

We came through wet to the arms and too weary for remark, only to encounter a labyrinth of alder. My spirits had been drowned in the dam. Distance was no longer enchanting, but downright painful. I had grown slippery. I fell and broke my arm, or almost did. Thornton laughed. So did I. There comes a time when the multiplicity of discomforts lies too deep for tears.

A half hour of this brought us opposite the cabin. The lake stretched around a bend for unbelievable distances. There was nothing to it but to swim across or to make them hear. We yelled, and no one appeared. We waded out and yelled again. It was a lovely evening. But the black flies were gormandizing upon our persons. We yelled. Presently a Christian emerged from the cabin and yelled back. Whatever he may have thought of human noises issuing from two amphibians, he lost no time in speculation. Within ten minutes we were dredged up into his boat, so to speak, and in twenty more were eating flapjacks and maple syrup out of his hand. The lake was Little Moose.

If those gentlemen who took us in plied us with towers of hot cakes and yards of trout, and shared their cabin and their clothes and their all without so much as a hidden smirk at the dazzling clownishness of our entrance—if those gentlemen should ever see this account, I hope they will realize again more directly than we could tell them, our appreciation of their hospitality. And not only that, but the great and impersonal service they rendered the law of the woods. At one time the Adirondacks seemed likely to become the private preserve of a few wealthy men, whose embargo upon stream and woodland was changing the prevailing spirit of good-fellowship into the bitterness of exile. Armed wardens, "no trespass" signs, unnecessary selfishness, aroused opposition, poaching, malice. The generosity of frontier life was speedily converted into suspicion and retaliation. The crisis came in murder and burning. And as quickly it subsided because of a change of front on the part of the capitalists and the State's acquiring a good deal of territory. The reaction is now complete. Campers are welcome anywhere. Permissions can be obtained for anything reasonable on the small holdings not already thrown promiscuously open. But best of all, the give and take, the natural hospitality has returned to stay. The stranger is cordially received and helped upon his way in the fashion of the remoter West. Our hosts were generous examples of the new spirit.

Little Moose Lake, encircled by forest and pro-

Photo by Warwick S. Carpenter

A LEGAL LEAN-TO FOR STATE LAND

THE CEDAR RIVER COUNTRY

tected by little mountains, is a spot to dream on. Deer come at dawn and dusk. Birds sing in the clearing. A spring issues near the one cabin. And from the cold lake flows a river filled with trout. If I did not feel that some reward was due the person who has read as far as this, Little Moose should remain undivulged. But I am reassured by the certainty that only the deserving will take the trouble to hie them thither.

Sleep washed away fatigue and the sting of past mistakes, and we awoke to the early beauty of an upland summer. It is astonishing how complete recuperation is in the free air. In the Great North Woods each day begins with a clean page, no matter how blotted the one before. The most complicated miseries untangle in a night, open to balsam healing, and good food and coffee revise untoward views of life. We blessed the mischances that had brought us to such a pitch of satisfaction, and we felt as if we had partly repaid our hosts who were leaving for Indian Lake by warning them of the corduroy.

As luck had it, our wanderings had been in the right direction, and lunch time saw us well down the right bank of Moose River, past Butter Brook and over a smaller unnamed stream which we christened Oleo with its own waters. We crossed Silver and were at the rendezvous. It was vacation ground for Diana. Three streams united to increase the Moose. It seemed as if no person had ever passed that way, so silent, so remote lay the sunny spaces. A generation ago some lumbermen cut out the hemlock. But it was a triumph for sensible cutting, and how different from the usual despoiling of timberland! As Lynn once remarked when we were confronted by a desolated tract,

"There 's a place for every lumber-hog, and every lumber-hog should be in his place." Lynn is not often profane.

Making camp in such a situation was an easy enterprise, and our camp, we flattered ourselves, should be more than a sop to the human instinct for a place to sleep. We had sheltered sunlight for the tent-site, balsam for the bed, firewood for all hours, a rill to drink from, a pool to plunge in, and a fisher's paradise radiating in three directions.

As the day waned we found ourselves listening for our partners. Shadows crept from the forest, the spruce spires glowed and went out. We prepared supper, and still they did not come. Night crouched about the fire, and many a time we thought that we heard our names when it was only the brook sounding through the stillness, the ripples breaking into consciousness.

Since both Lynn and Master Thomas were so wood-wise, we felt no alarm, and yet when we

THE CEDAR RIVER COUNTRY 75

heard an unmistakable shouting and saw them leading Luggins by the aid of a birch torch, we were relieved. There is more in the night forest than is dreamt of in any of our philosophies.

It was a tired, but triumphant quartet that rested in the balsam. And Luggins' old white face peered solemnly upon us, without comment, but obviously as of one who is digesting a new experience. He appeared ruminative, as if adding another to the memory of an already richly varied list of catastrophes. But Luggins was to have his reward. For the next five days we moored him upon a grassy island where he ate and dreamed delectably. At the end of the day he was glad to see us back from our excursions down the stream. Once he tried to tell us that he had smelled a bear. We found the tracks in the sand above our camp. But, all in all, the inertia of the life was beyond his criticism. Existence, for the moment, was justified.

And so was it for us. We were now utterly freed from the odor of our costermonger lives. Freedom was our plaything. Whether it was the forest spell or the mending of one's outfit, every sensation was vivid. We laid out long explorations for ourselves just to show that liberty should not make us soft. And on one of these we discovered Otter Brook.

Otter lies to the east of Little Moose, an hour's

travel for you who can keep the sun on the proper shoulder, but a year's wandering for those who will not mind their way. It is a stream of rocky reaches and great pools. The pools harbor some very large and proud trout who mutiny except under the command of the master angler. The conditions that fish propose before allowing themselves to be caught are preposterous. It is an art of pretense on both sides. But down the Otter there are other attractions if the fish remain perverse. First you travel along a diminutive canyon, and then suddenly the forest flattens out, stops, and you are out upon a natural meadow that lies greener than memories of Ireland. The forest rolls up the slopes of distant mountains, but before you, in extravagances of quiet and sunlight, the plains widen along the stream. And in a little while the Otter has joined the Moose.

The fact that there are a dozen other Otters and a dozen other Mooses in the Adirondacks cannot take the charm from this first of our discovery. It is a living matter of irritation, nevertheless, that the names of the myriad ponds should not be sorted out and shuffled a little better. The lakes and mountains were named by settlers who could have no ideas of the nomenclature prevailing in other places. When somebody killed a bear by a lake, the slaughter was commemorated by naming the water after the event. As there were a good many bears, there grew to be a good many Bear Ponds. There are six or seven now in the Adirondack Park. There are ten Clear Ponds, a dozen Wolf's, and fifteen Long ones. Deer Ponds, Pine Lakes, and the other inevitables flourish by the fives and tens. These cease to be names; they become disguises.

Of course it is rare that we come upon a region like Glacier Park ready and waiting to be christened by a geographical board. But there are beauties in the Adirondacks, quieter perhaps, but as suggestive as the proud title-bearers of Gunsight Pass and Two Medicine Lake, and it is a loss to everybody that their name is Mud. There are a dozen such.

Many places in the Adirondacks have names of distinction and some of charm—Massawepie, Raquette, Canachagala, Boreas, Crotched, Bonaparte, Joe Indian Pond, Honnedaga, Nehasane, Middle Brother Pond, Witchapple, Vly, T Lake, Nameless Creek, Squaw Brook, Paradox, Poke O' Moonshine—all these and some others have a personality that a succession of North Ponds necessarily relinquishes.

I have a conundrum. If you called Niagara, Johnson Falls, would its beauty be as great to you? Would you not rather date your letters from Witchapple than from Mud Pond?

Perhaps when the Conservation Commission has

made sure of all its real estate, and the timber, it may begin to conserve the beautiful heritage of Indian names that is fading from memory and the books. The sainted aborigines were the first American poets, and they deserve their Westminsters.

Strange to say the mountains fared better than the lakes. I dare say because there were so many of them that the average settler got discouraged; or his thoughts were so much more interested in his potato crop that he had little time to lift up his eyes unto the hills. He never climbed for either the altitude or the view. Discrimination was not necessary. Hence, instead of clumps of Blues and Greens over the landscape we have Wolf Jaws, Hurricane, Ampersand, Noon-Mark. These have nobility.

Those early summer days with Master Thomas and Thornton on the upper waters of the Moose pass my ability to mirror. The season had lost none of the delicacy of spring; the country was a fountain-land of life. Deer would step with care and grace down the rocky banks to drink. Wild ducks hustled their broods to safety. Beaver abounded; foxes barked; we knew that there was at least one bear in our vicinity. There was a largeness about the woods and the days that was satisfying. It was also disturbing. We longed to expand to it; we could not in full. Of the night

THE CEDAR RIVER COUNTRY

fires and philosophies, of the reticence and frankness nothing can be said, for the same tongue does not tell the dream and the interpretation thereof.

On a morning threatening thunder we broke camp. Master Thomas and his son were to return to Back Log for expected guests. Luggins, who had been belly-deep in the present for over-long, was to have his nose turned smartly to the future in company with Lynn's and mine. We saw our companions over Oleo and Butter dry-shod, and then, making sad jests, we parted. The idea of a book was now firm within us, and there was much country to be seen.

CHAPTER V

THE ADIRONDACK FOREST

A POET loves the forest most, a camper always, a lumberman for keeps. The great mantle of the Adirondack Mountains serves them all.

The goal of our desire, I remember, was to find ourselves in the forest primeval. We were always for pushing on into some denser growth that was indubitably primeval. So when we found that without knowing it we had spent a good part of a week in woods that had never been lumbered, we were considerably chagrined. We had expected, I suppose, a barricade of trees, so dark as to be eternal night, where gigantic trunks grew so close together that you could barely squeeze between.

But the primeval forest is far different. The original covering of the Adirondack slopes boasts occasional great trees, but they grow far apart. There is little undergrowth, though a wealth of moss and fern. Slash, burn, and thickets do not

Photo by Warwick S. Carpenter

AN ADIRONDACK LUMBER CAMP — 30 BELOW

THE ADIRONDACK FOREST

exist. There is a timelessness about it that new woods cannot assume. It is a magnificent sight or an interesting sight or a rare sight, depending upon whether you are intent on fashioning these trees into hexameters or backlogs or two-inch boards.

The artist sees a wonderland dripping with shades of green and gray and gold, roofed with spires and domes and black-groined arches, floored with the wildest profusion of ferned rocks and moss-grown trunks. He remembers it fragrant with the damp of twilight, alluring with its glimpses of dim aisles, silent always, always strange. He goes his way.

The camper finds it a spectacle for admiration and for groans. He responds to the fact of its greatness, but finds it not the most useful for his purpose. It is too wet, too large, too empty. But he returns.

The lumberman sees board-feet. He calculates great currencies moldering for lack of the ax. He regrets the moneys that stand unminted. The poet was melancholy by reason of the dim vastness and decay. The woodman's sadness is less vague. He realizes that but for the law he would have the land denuded in a winter. And when he has *his* will there is nothing to return to.

Of the forest that once covered the entire north about seventy thousand acres remain in the Park.

Seventy thousand acres come to about one third the Adirondack lake surface. Most of it is in the Essex County preserves; a little lies to the west of the railroad and the rest to the south of Indian Lake.

Of the rest of the park about one million four hundred thousand acres have been lumbered, but are covered with second or third growths. One hundred and twenty thousand acres are utterly denuded. More will still go, unfortunately, as the lumber companies hold twenty-three per cent. of all the Park land, and it is their rather shortsighted policy to take as much wood as possible and then let the land revert to the State for taxes. Of course in thirty years new trees can grow to a certain fullness if forest fires do not damage the soil beyond the repair of centuries. But thirty years is a generation.

These million and a half timbered acres would cover half of Connecticut. They offer a dozen kinds of trees in abundance, and a score of others scattered in small quantities. Besides this wealth of variety, numberless species of mosses, grasses, weeds, shrubs, and water-plants make the region a botanist's happy hunting ground.

In all this territory the white pine once reigned supreme. Within the Park boundaries now, however, it has sunk to fourth place in importance, and the new blister threatens to sweep it from the

THE ADIRONDACK FOREST 85

land as thoroughly as the chestnut has been swept from the Middle States. Of white pine standing, there remain seventy-five-million board feet.

The nearer it draws to the fate of the buffalo, the grander this tree seems, growing a diameter of over three feet, a height of more than fifty. Far off you can tell this magnificent tree by the droop of the long branches, and near at hand its five-fingered leaf bunches will make you sure. Beneath it the ground is always soft with needles, and above, its blue-green depths are always speaking with the winds. In some of the preserves magnificent groves of white pine are to be found. The trees on the Dug Mountain Ponds were glorious monarchs. To live in such company was to breath nobility.

The yellow pine in the Adirondacks is of inferior quality and lacks the patrician look of its white lord. As camper's fuel the pines are only fair, burning quickly to dead ashes.

Among the noblemen of the ancient wood the hemlock ranks high. There is about ten times as much of this left as of the white pine, but as it has been coveted and cut for wood and bark and root its days are numbered. The hemlock can easily be told from the other evergreens by the short flat leaves and firm-textured bark. Its shape and color mark it for appreciation. In the sunlight it takes on a soft, blue-green beauty that lends mystery to its dignity. Its fate is the leather tannery. The wood is hard to split.

Of all the conifers the spruce is the most numerous in the park. Two and a half billion board-feet still stand, despite the ravages of recurring pests and the perpetual pulp-wooder. There is no difficulty in telling the spruce, because its spiny leaves spiral about the branches and bristle thickly from the parent shaft. Its dark lances spike the air and on a winter day seem to stand like a cohort of centurions, with javelins ready. In the spring new tips of a delicious green spring from the end of every branch and relieve the ascetic appearance for a while. But the freshness soon passes, and the tree darkens into its habitual severity. Like most of the other softwoods, for a camper's fire spruce is scarcely worth cutting.

To all woodsmen the balsam is a friendly tree. Green, it will not burn, and seasoned, it burns too rapidly. But for generations of tired bodies it has furnished a soft and scented bed. It is easy to know. Its leaves are a little longer and broader than the spruce, and they do not grow around the stem, as do those of the spruce, but lie flat. They are lighter on the under side, and from them flows the odor of eternal youth. Not a billion board-feet remain within the Park.

Three other evergreens, the tamarack of the

swamp, the arbor-vitæ of the lake shore, and the red cedar, are present in appreciable quantities. Tamarack is excellent for backlogs and burns very slowly when green. Cedars burn to dead coals with considerable crackling.

The North Woods contain four and a half billion feet of soft woods and three and a quarter billion of hard, of which the birches, maples, beech, and poplar bulk the largest.

The white birch is the Adirondacker's chief reliance. There are few ponds along which it may not be found, growing in groups of threes and sevens; and one does not travel far in the deep wood without coming upon great ancestral trunks which are producing the best wet-weather tinder in the world. No storm is so protracted that some layer of the oily bark may not be found to burn, no situation so depressing that its sure aid for fire or shelter or canoe cannot relieve. Men have rescued themselves from nocturnal situations with the help of birch torches, boiled water in kettles of its bark, patched their worn foot-gear, or housed themselves in broad rippings from big trunks.

For burning, the yellow birch is better than its more spectacular white sister, and it even burns more vigorously green than dry. The black birch, much rarer than either, is the best of all. It does not claim superficial connection with its family, the bark resembling cherry, but its leaf gives it away. All three kinds split well. The white birch sticks—it is the winter occupation of the entire mountain region to cut and stuff them into stoves—look good enough to eat. About three quarters of a billion board-feet remain.

Of all the maples the sugar-maple leads in service and number and size. From the first it has been the homestead's friend. The maple has a sickly sound to us who are accustomed to the red and rubbishy specimens of our city streets. But to enter a great grove of sugar-trees is to renounce all prejudice.

The sugar-maple is known by its smaller leaf and larger bole. Although the maple family has no aristocracy of form, yet sometimes a sugar-tree will rise over a hundred feet and spread with a gigantic sweep. In the fall it glows in a red mound of color. Its wood makes fair fuel for the boiling of its sap.

In the northern Adirondacks the last week of a normal March sees groups of men and girls betake themselves to the sugar groves for the first festival of the year. The snow lies a foot or two deep in the forest; but during the forenoon and early afternoon the sun shines warm enough to set the sap running. At night the frost returns. It is this weather of alternate freeze and thaw that the country-side has waited for. Each

THE ADIRONDACK FOREST

tree over seven inches has been tapped with an iron spout on which hangs a pail. On good days the colorless, sweetish water drips constantly and fills the buckets faster than they can be collected from a grove of five hundred trees. A boy with a sledge, on which is a great container, drives around and collects the sap which is put into an evaporator. A fire drives off the water vapor, and as the sap runs down from vessel to vessel it slowly thickens. Before the scientific age, a great iron kettle did the whole trick, but less quickly, and the product was darker colored.

Presently the sap is taken into the shack and put in a flat receptacle on the stove. It bubbles over the birch fire like a lake of molasses taffy, and as it thickens the master sugar-man anxiously tests it in the snow. By this time the neighbors have been summoned, for this is the sugaring-off and very much of an occasion. At last the syrup is taken off the fire and stirred; little pans are filled with snow and each sweet-tooth sits about with one on his lap. A spoonful of the amber stuff is poured on the snow. It hardens instantly and is devoured as soon. There is no confection so pure, so delicate, so Edenish. There is no sociability so natural and so sincere as that which it instigates.

The warm syrup is strained through a piece of felt, and the dark remnant, called the sugar-

sign, is thrown away. The strained part is boiled again if sugar and not syrup is desired, and is put into molds to cool. In a fair year a tree will yield fifty quarts of sap, which boils down into two quarts of syrup, which makes one pound of sugar. This retails at twenty or at most twenty-five cents a pound. But as the sugar season comes at the time of least outdoor activity and as the utensils need be no more elaborate than one can afford, the industry still appeals to every one who retains a drop of colonial blood within his veins.

To Lynn and myself the circumstance of our first sugaring-off savored of the olden homespun days. We had been staying with LeGrand Hale in upper Keene Valley, and when the invitation went round that Mr. Lamb was to have a sugaring-off, we were included with that uncomputing hospitality of the big woods. From the little shack high on the hills the view swept in cloudy grandeur across the noble valley. Inside, around the stove, sat a dozen of the admirable: Mr. Hale, old, but straight and strong; the host, generous and jolly; his daughter, busy and gifted with an unlearned art of ease and modesty before these many men; George Beede, type of frontier youth, healthy and strong; other young fellows, quiet among their elders and before strangers, but with adventure lurking in their eyes. Blood never spoke more surely. It is such stock as this that will perpetuate the American tradition.

But to climb down from the sugar-maple, there is an insignificant and useless member of the family that thrives on wet land, called the swamp maple. But it claims one moment of the year. Late in August or early in September it flames for a brief day in scarlet, or vermilion. It is the first figure of the autumn pageant. There are three birches to the maple's one, the estimated board-feet being but a quarter billion.

Beech comes in a billion strong. Its smooth trunk of delicate gray, its exquisite foliage, and its burnability make it a favorite. Along with the sugar-maple and the rare hickory, it is an almost faultless fuel. When the beech goes, the wild animals will go, too, for there is scarcely one from the bear or the deer down to the chipmunk that does not depend upon its mast. In the autumn its gold and brown, and later its faded whiteness, are matters of distinction. The beech is an aristocrat.

The poplar, on the other hand, is essentially vulgar. It overtops most of the forest, though as yet it does not overtotal many species. It grows rank, blooms with a coarse flower, and decays into the yellow leaf early in the autumn, leaving a tall-boled awkward skeleton. Poplar is probably good for many things, but it burns worse than wet balsam when green. When dry, however, it is a fuel not to be despised.

The other trees of the Adirondacks do not grow in merchantable quantities. Alder is everywhere along the streams and it makes a good fire for a short stopping, but never grows to any great size. A scattering of oaks and basswood appears in the south where winds and birds have carried them. But nature's first idea was best, and today great quantities of the soft woods are being set out from the nurseries. Two million trees are planted every year.

At the outset there were three mortal conflicts that had to be waged by the Conservation Commission on a hundred fronts. The great park forest had to be protected from fire; the holdings of the lumber companies had to be protected from indiscriminate spoliation; the desert lands had to be reclaimed by plantings of many million trees, or some day not only all the fertility would be washed into the sea, but the water supply of the immense cities to the south would be endangered.

It takes thousands of years to make a soil, hundreds of years to grow a tree, and half an hour to destroy both utterly by fire. When the Commission came into power, the danger was encroaching upon the last stands of original forest. In Michigan four billion board-feet of timber had just gone up in one conflagration. Farther west

THE ADIRONDACK FOREST

whole Rhode Islands had been devastated in single fires. Railroads, cigarette-droppers, fishermen, malice, had combined to start one holocaust before the last was extinguished. In 1903, 688 fires, doing damage to the known extent of $864,082, burning 464,189 acres, and costing $153,763 to put out, were started, chiefly by carelessness. The Commission erected fire stations, cut fire lanes, paid fifty wardens to be on duty on mountain-tops with spy-glass and telephone, from the spring thaw till the autumn rains. This is the tale of their success. In 1914 there were 413 fires. But these were all extinguished for $13,978 before they had burned more than 13,837 acres to the tune of $14,905. During one summer the railroads were the cause of 120 fires, fishermen 125, hunters 90, smokers 220. It will require better spark arresters on engines, increased care among sportsmen, and more watchers before the double evil of the forest fire will be abolished.

The civic conscience grows so slowly that it is always worth while repeating the known, but undigested, fact that a forest fire burns the candle at both ends. The wood not only goes; the woods to come can never be. The seedlings, the seeds, and the soil are licked up; the unconsumed earth washes away; rivers are choked; droughts deepen in intensity, and floods double in violence; and the farmer, the paper user, the furniture-maker, and those who burn wood for fuel pay the indemnity. It is a tragic sequence. Yet it occurs because we never accept a fact until it begins to grab at our bank roll. This fact is edging up.

The Commission found that an unprotected forest was in as bad a way as an unprotected bank, subject to pillage and destruction. When the experts began to figure on the cost of protection they found, luckily, that the balance was on the proper side. The fifty wardens were not intended to conserve just an unproductive pleasure spectacle. They were guardians of a crop, as sure and even more constant than any cereal crop. The estimated annual crop of wood procurable from the Adirondack forest totals 250,000,000 board-feet. This is enough to construct an Atlantic City board walk from New York to Washington each year. And this is but the annual pruning from the Park trees from which the living forest would benefit. For it is known that the average decay throughout the year equals the year's growth.

The present rate of consumption is too great. We are not only living on our income, but eating into our principal as well. This rate amounted to 544,254,898 board-feet in 1901. This is equivalent to 3800 feet to the acre for 103,135 acres. This makes the handsome total of 161 square miles deforested a year. Such lumbering is bad enough,

Photo by Warwick S. Carpenter

PINES OF SARANAC

THE ADIRONDACK FOREST 97

but in addition the acids used in the preparation of pulp-wood are poured into the streams. Their poison kills the fish and sometimes the vegetation. And it is a commonplace of scientific measurement that the denudation of the forest lowers large streams and dries up small ones for part of every year.

In 1868, Verplanck Colvin, the explorer and far-sighted surveyor, made the first suggestion of a forest preserve. In 1873, he prophesied that "The Hudson River Valley must eventually contain one long marginal city, extending from the Mohawk River to New York. The Adirondack Wilderness is the only watershed which will afford a sufficient supply of pure water for such a population as will then exist."

In 1885, the Forest Preserve was at last organized. By 1902 it had secured control of 1,325,851 acres out of the Park's area of 3,226,144 acres. In the same year was incorporated a society, composed of landowners and others interested in maintaining the Adirondacks in their beauty of forest and water, in their abundance of game and fish; this society was called "The Association for the Preservation of the Adirondacks." It found much work at hand.

At that time in our national history, an era of great prosperity and of great rapacity was beginning. Individuals, small and great corporations, alike, had set their eyes in envy upon the riches remaining upon the Adirondack slopes. They desired to feast upon the wealth promised by water-power. Their influences working through Albany had just about paved the way for flooding unlimited areas of State lands. Other influences had all but amended the State constitution with the view to cutting down State forests. The title to much land had already been surrendered and much timber had already been deliberately stolen with the full knowledge of certain officials, when this Association came into being. For half a generation its labors have been ceaseless, and certain results that have been attained by it would have been lost, to the great detriment, if not wholesale destruction, of Adirondack resources, if its energy had been anything less than unflagging. To state some of its triumphs is to show how perilously close the great Park had come to utter spoliation.

This society has obtained an amendment to the constitution limiting the area of the forest preserve that might be flooded to three per cent.

It has advocated the retention by the State of title to State waters, because Verplanck Colvin's prophecy is coming true.

It has opposed the granting of State water-powers to private interests without compensation to the people.

It has opposed any amendment permitting the removal of live timber from the Forest Preserve.

It has taken measures to secure construction of fire trails in the Forest Preserve.

It has successfully employed engineers, lawyers, and detectives in order to keep informed of matters affecting public interests.

It has been instrumental in obtaining the recent bond issue of $7,500,000 for the purchase of Forest Preserve lands.

It has urged appropriations for replanting denuded areas.

It has exposed political graft. In 1905 it exposed the illegal removal of sixteen million board-feet of timber from State lands.

It has studied "top-lopping," fire-preventive inventions, and it helped to secure the substitution of oil-burning locomotives within the Forest Preserve.

It has sustained officials in the conscientious discharge of their duty, and has given legal as well as moral support to the State's forest administration.

It has enforced the law against illegal advertising signs on public highways of the Park.

It has retained expert advice in the study of forest taxation.

It has given publicity to the menace of ruthless hard-wood lumbering.

It is still trying to find a substitute for woodpulp in the manufacture of paper, which would relieve the vast forests that are being cut down each year to make newspapers.

By arranging conferences between lumber interests and conservationists, by lectures and unceasing propaganda, it has forwarded the ideals of Adirondack conservation.

Thanks to this Association, the great Park is still a park, still a refuge for wild game. Its members still subscribe large sums that the law may be kept over this woodland which is as large as three Delawares. And all their efforts will have result. Years from now when the Hudson is lined with cities and when three hundred million people live where now there are the fifty million, this magnificent playground will teach the stanch virtues that can be learned only in the wilderness. And the public-spirited members of the Association for the Preservation of the Adirondacks will have realized that they, in like manner with the Puritans and the heroes of '63, can be called the "Makers of America."

The days are coming wherein we shall again become aware of the forest. In the dim long ago the forest was a dark hinterland from which evil spirits came to prey and into which, glutted, they withdrew. Witches lived in the wood. Even today the dark aisles of the evening firs are shivery at nightfall because of these unchallengeable terrors of the past. Yesterday when out of the Adirondack ravines the cougar cried and the howl of the wolf sounded across the snow, the frontier children shuddered. Yet they liked to hear the legends of the wood.

But with the passing of yesterday the terrors abated. The frontier children grew up, reasoned themselves out of the witches, and shot the wolves. The forest ceased to be a thing of fear, of veneration, and became a matter of dollars and board-feet, a bank account in the rough. It was wantonly cut and criminally devoured by fire. This storehouse of legend, this temple of the race, was in danger of extinction.

Now all that is safely passed. We have let the buffalo go; we have barely saved the beaver, but we will save the forest. We will save it, not only for fuel, not only against flood, but because it is the most beautiful thing on the earth.

CHAPTER VI

THE RAQUETTE RIVER TRIP

MUCH study of the map had made us mad. The Adirondacks, a little clump of mountains in the northeast corner of New York State, had grown very large. This was because we had suddenly decided to see them thoroughly. We had already spent a month in their least conspicuous corner, with most of the spectacular and all the famous places yet to view. Lynn calculated that if we took a morning dip in each of the Park's lakes and ponds, we could make the round in about three years and seven months. To climb all the mountains would finish out the decade. Clearly to be thorough was to be preposterous. We decided to fish the still water on the Moose once more and talk things over. We fished, but did n't talk, and when shame of dead fish made us move, we were agreed upon the wisdom of a suggestion of Master Thomas's, to make a permanent camp on Raquette Lake, hire a canoe, and see the southwest Adirondacks from that base.

It was a matter of one day and two-and-twenty thunder showers to Raquette from the Moose.

Blithely did the southwest wind heave one blue cloud after another over the patient hills. There would be a rattle of thunder, and a flow of water would set in from the zenith. In ten minutes the gray curtain would be rolled away with considerable creaking, and we would come up for air. But nature being so very earnest, we were the more stirred to laughter. There is a certain imbecility about my nature that will crop out on serious occasions, and Luggins was very serious. Such phenomena had never figured in his Western life. A rain was one thing, but spasmodic drownings were another.

To come upon Raquette gipsy-wise is to surprise the essence of beauty. Not many have the fortune, for the lake is famous, touristed. Thousands of people in a season are shunted off the main line at Clearwater and, after leaving deposits of trunks and picnickers along the Fulton Chain, arrive at breakfast-time at the Raquette terminus. Then a launch deports them to the hotels and camps to enjoy the summer. It is the same system to which all picturesque localities are subjected sooner or later and to which most in the end succumb. But Raquette's beauty has not been ruined yet, in fact, it is hardly marred.

At the wildest end, called North Bay on the maps, we settled down to a more ambitious housekeeping than any yet attempted. A tiny cove made the coziness absent from a larger waterside. Niggerhead Mountain* rose behind and made a black beacon to steer for in the dark. The view from our supper table showed long, wooded capes, wide lake arms and a rare sky-line. The shores of the lake are high and overhung with old trees, and the length of shore-line is well on toward a hundred miles. Much of the land is held by the State, and that owned privately is fitly administered. Some of the great estates have established havens of luxury, but the reaches of water are so great that these log palaces are perfectly in keeping.

On all sides hills run back from the lake and many of them are mountains that stand up proudly. There is one eminence, called the Crags, that is specially worth the fifteen minutes' climb. From it one gets the entrancing contour and colors of the lake. Yet it is so low that the intimate loveliness of things lingers in the memory when the delight of views from more exaggerated heights is but a blur.

After a month of trail, a canoe was refreshing, and we were soon planning trips of two or three nights away from our base, a luxury of choice presenting. Raquette is the paddlers' paradise. You can go up to the head of the Fulton Chain, or down to Saranac and around by Tupper and the Forkeds, or over to Blue and indulge in only

---

*[This offensive name later disappeared from state maps. *Ed.*]

Photo by Warwick S. Carpenter

The Three-Minute Tent

negligible carries. We began with Blue. And since two Boy Scouts had the benevolence to be camping near us, we loaned them the care of Luggins with a pittance for amiability's sake. They were downright good fellows, as Scouts usually are, and said that they didn't mind having a horse about the house. Of course Luggins insisted on very little entertaining.

To set out in a light canoe under a fair heaven and with a good wind on the shoulder is to taste translation; and it was a stirring breeze from the north that set us briskly on our way. The waters of Raquette are so cut that only under the stiffest blows are they unmanageable, yet there are stretches, particularly with a west wind, that lead the stern paddle to admire himself if he comes through with a dry boat. Thanks to Lynn's unweakening vigilance, we kept our fidelity to an upright keel, and in a shorter time than we'll ever do it again, slid into the flawless waters of the Marion.

The Marion is one of those astonishing Adirondack streams that you cannot call a river because it seems not to flow and yet which you dare not call a flow because there is some current. It winds so painstakingly that Lynn said that there must be alcohol in the water. Yet in the middle of the windingest place we nearly jumped out of the canoe on being confronted by an impertinent steamer. There it was pumping around the corners, as amiable as a dachshund. It conveys the public from the Raquette Railway to Blue Mountain. It is a forgivingly quiet little boat.

Right in the middle of this amazing trip we boarded a toy railroad, canoe and all, and were set down by Utowana Lake, which merges into Eagle, which merges into Blue. And if you are as tired as we were, you will not climb the mountain on the afternoon you arrive.

Blue Mountain Lake is most beautiful viewed from half-way up its mountain. From there it is a gem. Close at hand it is a gem still, but its setting has been tamed a bit. It does exist slightly for the hotel; it should exist wholly for the mountain. But I have to admit that that is what Lynn calls transcendental raving and a bit unreasonable. The lake to-day is gemlike enough. Lovely islands venture out from wooded shores. The sights of housekeeping upon its capes are cunningly concealed by an arras of green. And the guardian mountain asserts its guardianship with dignity.

The climb added very little to our knowledge of the wilderness because one of the white clouds that had been piling up suddenly toppled over upon the summit and us. And when we crawled out of the debris of lightning, thunder, and hail, we could see that the rain was raining all around for considerable distances as in the Stevenson poem.

We met a man on the way down, also abandoning the bath, who told us that while extensive, there was nothing unique about the view. His opinion I have heard repeated by others. Blue stands about two thousand feet above its lake, which is about as much above the sea. On all sides there must be a notable look-off into the ridgy west and toward the mountainous north, but the big peaks are so far away that the view leaves an absentee impression, I am told.

The only unfortunate circumstance about asking information is that you get too much. Our informer, whom we had picked up at the three-thousand-foot level, had a freshness of interest that was astonishing in one of his years. He had the appearance and endurance of a German spy, and if it had been the year for German spies we should have counted ourselves in fortune. But he knew too much about the war. In fact, he knew everything about it. Although the war was just ending its second year, it had been conducted with so much variety and vivacity that there was a good deal to know; yet he knew it all and told us about it. Perhaps our appearance warranted it. There is a chance that our clothing, bedraggled with the now bankrupted cloud, or our faces (not too intelligent at their best and now unshaven) begged to be brought up to date. The stranger made the most of the supposition.

We had got only to the merits of the Gallipoli campaign when we reached the lake. It had been very historic, but fatiguing and we were in terror lest the gentleman should offer to finish the war while we paddled him around the lake. The afternoon was turning fine. It was a critical moment. But there was no breeze to speak of, and the black flies, the punkies, the mosquitos, and the assorted gnats, seeing us standing about the boat in delicate attitudes, joined the party informally. At first our instructor would only pause in his exposition for a moment to slap. We did nothing to frighten them off. Soon the narrative flagged for longer, but none the less industrious, intervals. They were biting deliciously. He fled. Lynn grinned as he looked affectionately at the mosquitos eating his bare arm. "We couldn't hurt 'em after that," he said. The boat shot out on the lake, and we were rid of all the bores without bloodshed.

There was not much use for Luggins at Raquette. Therefore he enjoyed the place: it is a pleasant thing to make everybody happy. But we decided, on the Scouts' advice, to harness him once more in a jaunt to the back country, including West Mountain, an eminence of not quite three thousand feet and one which we would not have bothered with except for their remark, "It's the

THE RAQUETTE RIVER TRIP

bulliest little view in the country, and don't you forget Shallow, either.''

Skirting the shores of North Bay to the West Mountain trail (which is fairly well marked from the west side of the lake nearest the mountain) was a recrudescence of frontier life. If we had been commandeered for the task, we would have reproached our officers as singular fools. But as it was a voluntary venture, we complimented our pertinacity and plugged on. Only Luggins' compliments were doubtful. There would be an open space of great trees, then a ravine overgrown with alders and black flies, then a short scramble through moss and a repeat. But we had waited for exactly the right day and after we had struck the trail, we progressed swimmingly.

The first twenty minutes of the trail is boggy; the second twenty undulates through lifting woods of birch and spruce, and the last forty, which is the climb, tries not good brawn, but harries somewhat the over-corpulent. Out West we had led our horse up and down natural ladders that Jacob would have liked to reconsider. But Luggins was always game. No matter how diffident was his attitude toward the ordinary occupations of the road, when confronted with something serious, the blood of his sporting ancestry simmered in his veins. The more crushing the predicament, the gamer he got. Otherwise we would have been fools, indeed. I am thus explicit lest somebody try to out-Hannibal us with a mere livery-stable nag. Nothing but impossible luck would prevent such an animal's address remaining permanently, "The Woods." It takes Western experience to teach a horse not to break its leg in mossy pitfalls. With one to pull and another to prod you can get a pony up anything short of a precipice; it is the down-grade grave that yawns.

All this is not intended to convey that the ascent of West was hard. There was scarcely a rod not practicable for a nurse and a baby-carriage. There was one rod. We had sat down to let Luggins recapture his wind and we had sat too indiscriminately. It was a place set aside in the divine plan for some yellow-jackets and for them only. They stood upon their rights, and we stood not upon the order of our going. I have never seen Luggins more agreeable to the suggestion of speed. He disappeared into the moose bushes in an angry splash of green. Lynn made an emotional gesture and dove after him. I followed under the strongest convictions. I don't know why the Scouts had not told us of that place. Such neglect lessened the value of the movement in our eyes for a while. Inquiring tourists can locate that nest by looking carefully for a deceitful trail that branches from the main trail on the left as you ascend. The trail has to be noticed for the descent anyway, as it is sure to mislead you and you might just as well have the yellow-jackets in mind at the same time. They have staked their claim just a few yards above the fork. If there is any doubt look for a blue bandana that I dropped in the briskness of my departure. I am sure it is there.

Although it was high noon and after when we reached the bare top, the day had still the freshness of creation upon it. A world of green ranges fell away from all sides, and on all sides lay the blue and glitter of much water. Raquette seemed everywhere, and a score of outer lakes ringed us round with their effect of calm and waiting. Crisp white cloudlets floated at serene heights, and here and there threw the panorama into shadow. The wind came so gently from the north that it was comfortable to have our tea and mush and raisins on the summit. The outspread peacefulness grooved itself into our sensibilities, and I need but to close my eyes to recover the scene, so white and blue under the caressing sun. A moment of such content is worth a mountain of preparation; or rather each for the other. And when you add to the fair universe yonder a comprehending friend at hand, you have the best of life's adventures. We proved that we knew how to live in heaven by quitting the summit in good time.

The exploration now began. The Scouts had

mentioned Big Moose Lake, but we knew from previous inquiry that Big Moose was the abiding place of fortune while Master Thomas had told us about the Brandreth trout. Besides, it was trailless thither, and we were still ambitious.

It was slow, but not painful progress that we made down into the great green bowl below. Wilderness advance is measured variously. About the only unit never taken is the mile. On corduroy I suspect that travel would be registered by the oath. Ordinary snow-shoe climbing can count at least a mile an hour. The airman counts his flight by States. And we with Luggins, at times negotiating ledges and at others traversing beech groves, with abandon, felt that a mile an hour was not too disastrous a speed. As yet time was no particular object and place absolutely none; so we neither urged Luggins to the verge of eternity nor let him dawdle. We made our first camp beneath some pines with a brook to guard the fire, and slept where no one had ever slept before.

Trout-fishing with a horse was a new and possibly not an unrivaled enjoyment. We tried various combinations: tying him up and going back for him, leading him on and fishing up to him, dividing the pleasure of being groom by the watch. If Brandreth had not really been more than a mere earthly trout-stream has a right to be, we

Photo by Warwick S. Carpenter

NAMELESS CREEK

THE RAQUETTE RIVER TRIP

must have shot Luggins from sheer vexation and carried out our kitchen on our backs. But Brandreth would have restored the temper of a dyspeptic. Beautiful pools, beautiful trout, beautiful bugs! We began with cursings, but concluded with pity, for as the day wore on so did the flies. We covered Luggins's flanks, but that only drove them to his fore. To us protected by science and enlivened by great luck, the blacks were of a negligible interest. But to Luggins, with nothing to think about except his station in a mismanaged world, they were humiliating. Finally we made a glorified smudge on each side of him and set off down the stream with easy consciences. Youth and love and Italy was, as a combination, utterly flat compared to youth and late afternoon on Brandreth when the trout were rising. The Scouts had done a good turn the day that they told us of West Mountain and the regions beyond.

After consideration of the calendar we gave up the notion of doing the Fulton Chain. Perhaps the nearness of Brandreth to our camp on North Bay had something to do with it, but our imaginations had more. The Fulton Chain is a navigable string of lakes dedicated to the summerer. He lines their banks. His victrolas fill in the natural vacancies of an evening in the woods. His womenfolk enjoy themselves shrilly. Not that the summerer is not a good sign. He is an earnest of the day when "God's green caravanserai" shall supplant the more popular summer hotel. There is everything to be said for the summer camper, no matter how clumsy or how careless of his tin cans. May his tribe increase! But also may it not overrun the lovelier wilderness until it shall have learned to put out its fires and to bury its cans.

For the beginning Adirondacker the Fulton Chain sounds like a very training school. Stores are not so far apart that you will suffer if you've left the ax at home. Steamers are at hand to pick you up if blistered. The carries are supplied with carriers if your pride goeth before a haul. And the railroad folders say that "brook trout, lake trout, whitefish, and bass inhabit these waters." It does not say how closely, however. I should judge that sparsely would be a good adverb.

The Fulton section of the Adirondacks centering about Old Forge is about the oldest of the sportsman's retreats. It was from this region that the game getters went out to kill the last elk, the last moose, and the last wolf. Even yet the winter season in this section is not unreminiscent of the good old days, for in winter the voice of the summer maiden is gone, the tan of the bank clerk is fading in the city movies, and the Old Forger's

THE RAQUETTE RIVER TRIP 119

age-long occupation of sitting by the stove has recommenced for another eight months.

We did, however, paddle down Brown's Tract Inlet, which is the last stage of the voyage from Old Forge to Raquette, and we can recommend it as an auspicious opening to the major pleasures of the lake. We also walked into Shallow, which calls forth memories of raspberries, deer, and frogs. Part of the trail is in a deserted lumber road, lined with bushes that shed red lusciousness into eager hands. It is a strong-minded person who can quit that road in good health.

Shallow is a pond of hospitable dimensions, yet so withdrawn as to gladden a hermit's heart. We were lucky enough to discover a leaky, but floatable craft which ferried us to an ideal spot for a camp on the side farthest from the trail-end. Tall pines gave play to the breeze, and birch and balsam offered their best. Behind us thick woods built up a strictest privacy where dusk skulked forever.

A creek, called Nameless, saunters into the pond at the west end, and on the pavement of lily-pads at its mouth we caught supper. Ah! Delicious legs. They grew long and meaty at the nether extremities of croakers whose self-satisfaction was their undoing. No art was needed to procure them. You tickled their throats with a bare fishhook and when it was in the right position jerked. If it was an unsuccessful jerk, the frog gave you another try. I have never seen anything more idiotically satisfactory, even if it was not art.

While we were preparing supper and the odor of the frying-pan rose to heaven, the deer began to appear on the grassy beaches half a mile away. The sun, which had set for us, still shone for them. They roamed placidly and fed at ease. Deer have not good sight, as we proved by getting into our absurd shallop and poling toward them. Halfway over one raised its head and went on feeding. Soon the three began to move restlessly along the margin. But we had got within sixty yards before they jumped the bushes and were gone. In a decent canoe we could have halved that distance and perhaps better. Master Thomas has told me that in one hot August afternoon he has counted twenty-seven deer on the shores of Shallow. Large preserves lie near the pond, and the deer are far more numerous than in the east.

Nameless Creek is an artist's lure. At twilight it winds in blackness of shadow between skeletons of drowned trees. The darkness and silence of the forest were heavy. One is almost glad to get back to a fire from so eerie and lonesome a lagoon. But in the sunlight it is enchanting. Spruce files stand in along the sides. There is often the stir of some kingfisher, and the rounded clouds float flawless beneath you. There are two skies.

Such a place demands comradeship. It is an easy pleasure to spend the day fishing down a mountain brook alone. But Nameless is too aloof, the gaunt and naked trees too taciturn. Lynn felt the same as I about it. We both confessed to a relief in coming out upon the pond. To call the place "Nameless" was an inspiration.

And while I am on the question of influences, I would like to add my testimony concerning that enigmatic sensation, the fear of the dark. Why, do you suppose, that two grown men, who have deliberately fled the great white ways because of the enjoyment of the great unlighted,—why should they prefer to stick around the camp-fire after dark? Once I slept alone in the woods for two months and at the end of that time I was no more broken from the faint distrust of something beyond the firelight than at the beginning. It was the safest place in the world, my Adirondack camp. There were no dangerous animals, no dangerous insects, no snakes, no tramps. I took supper regularly with friends on the other side of a lake, paddled over alone under glorious heavens, and suffered no feeling of the nerves. But my tent was fifty feet back from the water's edge, and those fifty feet through darkness up the familiar path verged on the unpleasant. If they had been more unpleasant I should have left a lantern at the landing to light me home, but that seemed childish.

There was always a relief when I had lighted the lantern in my tent—a very slight relief, but actual. I never thought about being alone after the light was burning or minded waking up at night. I would like to know whether forest rangers, Yellowstone guards, night watchmen and all the citizens whose legal business is conducted after dark, have this same faint distrust of it that is many degrees less than fright, yet a shade different from daylight ease. All our cave-men ancestors could not have been arrant cowards, lying in mortal terror at the approach of twilight. Yet anything short of that could scarcely have survived as instinct when so many other instincts have fallen by the way. On the other hand, if it be imagination, it should be controllable and not involuntary. Children are brave by nature, yet they suffer most. There are more things in heaven and earth and in the dark, than are dreamt of in our philosophies, Horatio.

There was one trip about which we had often talked, the famous Raquette River loop, which our Scouts, by taking charge of Luggins, made possible for us. As High Lords of the Stable they had won the confidence of Lynn on the occasion of our excursion to Blue. Unfortunately they were going to break camp on the fifth morning, which gave us just four days for the hundred-mile circuit. But it was too good a chance to lose, and

THE RAQUETTE RIVER TRIP

we made our getaway at six-thirty under the best auspices of wind and sky. Ten days of canoeing had made us fit.

In the northeastern part of our country there are many celebrated sequences of lake and stream which sportsmen have extolled; some because the scenery is a little wilder, some because the fish are a little bigger. In Canada there are more lakes than there are outdoor men to use them. But I can think of none where you can make a circle with so little portaging through country constantly varying, but always beautiful. To the woods-lover it is enough to be in the forest. One does not need to laud one section more than another. There is no city on our continent that cannot offer at the end of a trolley some of the charms of nature. And so it shall not be my care, advertisement-wise, to magnify our days upon the Raquette. The Rangeleys may be more exciting and Algonquin Park more wild. I hope some day to visit both. But on the Raquette the nights are just as mysterious, the spruce-lands just as alluring, the spell of the twilight just as subtle, the wandering odors just as sweet as in more distant wildernesses. Go see for yourself.

The broad bay, leading out of Raquette on the northeast, draws the south wind beautifully on a summer morning. Gaily we blew before it. We did not know in great detail what lay before us, but we did know that the distance approximated a hundred miles, and that we had about a hundred hours to spend. It may not be the ideal way to set out upon an excursion, but there was a certain novelty and stimulus in being limited. We puritan progenies do thrive upon goals and disciplines.

The rounded hills slipped steadily by, and we removed our ascetic stores for the carry to Forked Lake with the feeling that we had hardly got under way, although Luggins was already five miles to the rear. Half a mile of road and we were re-embarked.

Forked is an ingratiating lake. From its shores rise great rocks, and behind them stand worthy trees, and all the while long arms beckon to be explored. But we promised ourselves another visit and paddled on.

The Raquette River reassumes its identity after issuing from Forked Lake; it even stands upon its dignity as a river and demands some obeisance in the form of carries. There is a long mile and a half carry around impossible water which a wagon will perform for you for a dollar and a half. With a horse waiting to be asked, to carry your own boat seems like too gratuitous sweating. At the farther end your lunch will nestle gratefully in its appointed place. But we held out for another half mile, preferring to eat ours near the sound of Buttermilk Falls.

Log Drive on the Raquette River

Photo by Warwick S. Carpenter

THE RAQUETTE RIVER TRIP

Buttermilk is quite a decent cascade. In one of Adirondack Murray's tales, a guide (either somnambulant or full of whiskey) is supposed to go over it in a boat and survive. Murray claimed that the exploit was founded on fact. It is difficult to believe, and as Lynn remarked, "Buttermilk and whiskey must be a mighty fetchin' concoction, but he 'd rather take his straight." The late thunder storms had loaned volume to the falls. They churned up a curtain of mist and roared handsomely. We gave our digestion its due beside this tumult. But though the spectacle, the overflow of fifty ponds, begged continually for one look more, Long Lake lay a little way ahead, with but a half-mile carry intervening.

Of Long Lake I am ashamed to say that I remember almost nothing. There remains a blurred picture of a ribbon of water, a bridge appearing remotely ahead, enlarging, drawing close enough till its spidery rods shone in the sun, then passing into the unconsidered rearward. I remember the picture of low hills, points that loomed ahead, jutted at us, and fell by. Chiefly, however, remains the exhilaration of the paddle. It was a warm day, and the southwest wind held steady. A glance at the map will show you what that meant to us. It meant almost aviation in a light canoe. The little waves curled in exasperation, but could not keep up. Speed was no effort. Long Lake is fourteen miles in length on paper. With the wind it is four, against it forty. To have bucked that breeze a whole afternoon would have made fit penance for the damned. To fly with it was exhilaration. Air-travel, I foresee, will leave few memoirs.

Long Lake is too desirable to be dismissed with a hazy word. It is the geographical axis of the Park. To the south and the west and the north lies an intricacy of waterway that a generation of vacations could scarcely master. To the northeast rise the Giants Clothed with Stone, five hundred square miles of them. Park lands and private preserves guarantee the length and breadth of all this beauty. I am beginning to regret that southwest wind.

With the excitement over, we began to feel fatigue, and soon after entering the Raquette, found a camping place. The summer was getting on, and twilight coming earlier now, and before we had the night wood gathered, bright sheaves of the aurora wavered up into the northern skies. The banners of light advanced beyond the zenith. Shadows of white flame quivered and disappeared; cold, aloof, spiritual, and intense. And when the aërial signaling was done, and the streamers had ceased their flying, the white glow along the north still lighted the forest eerily. It was like the reflection from some great celebration of which we

THE RAQUETTE RIVER TRIP

had not heard. It was something to have seen from the outside. Some day we would know. Down we laid us, with all our muscles murmuring content, and almost before we had taken the last turn, the sun of morning was shining under the tent's gray hood.

Having made such unpredicted progress on the day before, we were now in a position to take the longer route, which included Upper Saranac. If we had been pressed for time, the alternative would have been to follow the Raquette around to the Tuppers.

The day began smoothly with five winding miles down the easy stream. Then came a long carry (also a dollar and a half) around white water and some falls, with a farewell to the river at Axton. A lift over into a small pair of lakes, the Spectacles, a half mile of carry and we ate belated lunch at the bottom end of Upper Saranac.

Saranac is a very beautiful sheet of water, pierced by a hundred wooded promontories, furnishing a hundred charming vistas. But for men hunting rest, it is hardly satisfying. At the end of every vista there is a "no trespassing" sign, actual or implied. Every promontory gives a reason for moving on. Saranac is no longer a part of the wilderness; it is a pleasure-land of great beauty. If you recognize this at the outset, there will be no disappointment. There is plenty of wilderness elsewhere, and one must not begrudge, but congratulate the millionaires upon their architects. Nature has been educated to perfect taste. The lake is eight miles long, and unless you try to find a place for your tent, you would never guess how expensive.

At the head of Saranac stands the Inn, from the porch of which an exquisitely modulated view of hill and headland and level waters is to be had. On the porch the remote world of lovely dresses and afternoon tea was going round. We had forgotten that there was any reality but ours. It was something of a shock. We hurried around to the kitchen door for some supplies.

Of one thing I am sure: the joys of the road are very real, and so are the joys of the Ritz, but you cannot oscillate from one to the other too rapidly and enjoy it. For weeks on end a fellow may elect to do his own cooking, to dress in woolens, to wander light-heartedly through dust and misadventure, with the whole system of luxury and equipage forgotten and undesired. He may also breakfast at ten, golf in white flannels, dine to music and the converse of fair ladies, and never feel an itch to wash the dishes or sleep out in the rain. It is habit that hardens you to either. But this is the point: you have to take these moods in big splashes and not too thinly sandwiched. You dare not alternate luxury and the Spartan life too

THE RAQUETTE RIVER TRIP 131

rapidly, or you will be calling yourself regretful names.

Now Lynn and I were far from ready for the big exchange, so we bought our chops and chocolate in high disdain of white napery and *hors-d'œuvres*. We left the ladies on their porch as unenvious as cold potatoes. While doubtless they, using our sad case to make a moment's conversation, wondered what pleasure we could find in spoiling food and sleeping on the ground. It is the old question of age and the red gods.

It was not easy to find a place to camp where we could trespass in comfort and safety at the same time. But we finally Robin-Hooded ourselves under the greenwood half-way down the lake. I trust that our absentee landlord heard the prayers we raised to his forbearance. But there are intruders and intruders, and the latter have to suffer for the former. In this connection I have a story that is absurd, but true. On the grounds of the Placid Club stands a grove of white birches, whose beauty was radiant. Some strangers of the summer race passed by and coveted and cut, utterly regardless of private property or the injury to the trees. They wanted the bark; the girdled trees might die. When the crime was discovered, the club painted the eyesore white in an effort to save the trees as well as to preserve their looks. It was too cleverly done. Not a month had passed before another party of uninvited picnickers was seen actually endeavoring to remove the counterfeit. There is a rapacity that o'erleaps itself: these picnickers were fined. It would make an interesting study of national growth, the statistics of vacations. The cramped city-dweller is the man who needs nature most and the last to take to the woods. He commits the most grotesque trespasses. He does not understand their spirit.

Offense comes from every creed and condition of man. And the amount of selfishness perpetrated by the passer-by is enraging. The holiday season is marked by a litter of past lunches. Smoldering cigarettes and unextinguished matches ruin men's estates with a sickening finality. It is small wonder when one's holdings are kept unharmed only at the expense of perpetual vigilance that landowners should limit their courtesies. They are really remarkably generous. A camper with a reputation for carefulness with fire can obtain almost any privilege. Perhaps another generation of training will eliminate the vacation hog.

But let the transitory grouch disappear in the odor of broiled chop. For some time we had subsisted on epicurean dishes, trout in all its manifestations. Lynn had embellished our meatless days until there was no virtue in them. However, when we did find ourselves sitting before the little sizzlers and when we did sink our incisors into the crusted fat, two vegetarian votes were lost. The relish of some meals lives after them. I have not as yet established a full sympathy with our ancestors of the cavern who ate their meat on the hoof, despite its scientific advantages. But that evening's satisfaction will not be soon forgotten. We did not bother with forks. We had neglected to hunt for them till the chops were getting cold. It taught us a lesson of the good old pre-utensil days: that a chop in the hand is worth two on the plate. You have heard of gnawing hunger. Well, we gnawed, and if that be brutish, then I am in perfect accord with the dumb animals.

The third day, of varied memory, dawned fair. But the gods, thus far so heavily in our favor, were turning neutral. A south wind made the four miles down to the Sweeney carry an exhibition of early morning vigor, and when we arrived, Sweeney or his descendant was not to be discovered. The carry was three miles, however, and transportation was worth a good deal of waiting. Yet when the transportation company did come, he said that he was engaged by another party.

Money is the resource of those who lack the more spiritual persuasions, I suppose. So, as a confession of weakness, we offered him money.

It was rather dreadful, but we argued that in all probability this other party was not being patiently awaited by a packhorse and two amateur horse-keepers, and that therefore his errand could not be as urgent as ours. The carrier thought the same for two dollars extra.

It was late in the morning when we were fairly on our way, and there were still fifty complicated miles ahead of us. The south wind increased manfully, and the heat beat upon us, but every stroke was bringing us nearer home, and we said little. At times the country opened to rolling vistas dominated by Mount Morris. At times the forest closed about us. We met nobody and had no adventure of note, and our first stop was before the swift water eight miles or so below the carry, where we quieted our feelings with a slim tea and a promise of a generous supper.

Below, about fifteen minutes, if you will look for another channel on the map, you will find a decided short cut, and almost immediately you come out on Big Simon's Pond. We didn't stop to inquire who Big Simon was, but set to work using his pond without permission and with all the energy at our command. Very soon we came around the bend and were confronted by our worst fears. It was to be a lively afternoon.

Looking back upon it, I believe that the big wind was a help. Every moment was a sparkling

Photo by Warwick S. Carpenter

THE LONG LAKE COUNTRY

THE RAQUETTE RIVER TRIP

uncertainty, and the fun of it relieved the toil. The canoe was light; Lynn was skill itself; the waves were playful rather than dangerous as long as we observed ordinary caution. But just before we landed, after it was all over but the shouting, I suddenly realized that it had been a day's work. The sun was almost of the same opinion. But not so the map. There was a giant carry ahead of us, three miles of it at least, and this time no charioteer was waiting to be conjured forth even by all the money in the township. For now we had been insensibly drawn back into the wilds. The influence of the village at the upper end of Big Tupper did not reach so far. We had no other's strength to rely on.

How people accomplish things alone I do not see. It was because Lynn was there (to whom I could not explain that I was weary to the marrow and that life was disagreeably pointless anyway) that I began to tie the paddles for the portage. Or rather it was because Lynn was Lynn. I know many a good soul before whom I would have no particular hesitancy in lying down and dying. They are good to dine with and to sit with through the play. But I cannot conceive of them leading me into action. And what is comradeship for if it is not the thing that makes the extra mile possible?

As usual we did our hard work in silence, and

as usual it proved less wearing than our fears.
To be sure the light did almost fail us. To be
sure I got so tired that I could make progress with
the boat only by dint of counting sixties, planning
things to eat, and other mental makeshifts. Three
miles isn't much if you spell each other off by
the watch, but it is a great thing to have behind
you. And when it was over, we suddenly remembered our noon-time promise of a big meal.

We remembered it, but neither of us mentioned
it.

"I think I'd like a little tea," Lynn murmured
from the patch of sand where he lay blinking at the
first star.

"With the fresh loaf and apple sauce," I added
from the flat of my back. My foot, I think, was
half way in the lake where it had fallen.

We had carried the dried apples by every meal,
saying that we'd find a better use for them yet.
It is a filling, tasty, good-to-go-to-bed-on dish, is
apple sauce, delicately sweetened and eaten with
new bread. Up we got to put the kettle on. And
then the tragedy happened. The plates were got,
our palates primed, our bodies propped for the
final labor of eating, and we found that one of
us (no matter which) had sweetened our *piece de
résistance* with corn meal. The result was mostly
de résistance.

That evening we broke every law of our own

decalogue. Instead of making bed, we scooped out hollows in the sand. Instead of making a night fire, we relied upon the season's not betraying us. Instead of putting up the tent, we put it under. And, I might as well add, instead of sleeping, we dozed off from time to time.

Yet from that same sand bank I carry to this day three pictures that my memory loves to look on. One was of late evening. A quarter moon was just disappearing behind the black wall of spruces, and the shores of the little lake seemed very still. The next must have been after midnight. It was much colder and wreaths of mist were curling from the pond; a loon was calling from the farther shore. Lynn was sleeping, his arm thrown back over his fine head. I lay down again, the forsaken call, the vapors of the lake, and the breath of Lethe winding round my heart.

The last picture was too beautiful for fully waking eyes. The sun had not risen, but had sent scarlet and orange streamers to proclaim his coming. The pond lay breathless in the coils of mist. Except for the lad beside me, there was no hint of life. It was creation over again. And then he stirred, opened his eyes, saw me awake, and said, yawning:

"We're damned fond of Luggins, don't you think?"

The day had come on which we had pledged

ourselves to lighten our Scouts of their responsibility, and we were five carries and six lakes from home. But the spite had left the south wind, and we attacked the carries with precision. While Lynn tied the paddles crisscross for a shoulder rest, I assembled the other articles. If it was his turn with the canoe, I helped him up with it, got under the big duffel bag, slung the other over it, carried the ax in one hand, the rods in the other, and led the way. It took two minutes to get started and two to reassemble the things in the boat, count them, and push on. "Business as usual" was our slogan, and the little carries became not pestiferous, but amusing. As for the aches of yesterday, they had vanished with the morning mists. It had become a pleasure jaunt again. There is something so reviving in being immersed in the air of forests that the amount of actual slumber does n't matter much.

We were now traveling through the great Whitney Preserve. Deer herded on the shores of the little ponds. They did not always bother to run away. Loons swam a little to one side and went on fishing. We were so tuned down to the natural key that we vibrated with pleasure to the commonest things. Could the woods have performed a greater service? By shedding starch and five-course meals and the chauffeur, one finds the luxury of flannel shirts and the taste of food and the mastery of the wheel. Think, then, what discoveries lie in wait for the man who can keep the best of *each* variety of life. It is the middle course that makes the slipperiest riding. Extremes are easy. It is easy to succumb to the lazy life of the log cabin or to the schedules of citizen routine. In one sphere you do not think at all; in the other your thinking is done for you; the result of either is listlessness. But to carry your mental stimulants to the woods or to bring your woods health and simplicities to town is to improve upon content. It is to create a new world for most of us.

The flaring morn had been portentous of changing weather, and as we entered Forked Lake at its northernmost projection, the sun yielded to the steadily thickening cloud. The dark high shores of that enchanted water were close about us; no wind stirred; the afternoon darkened. The foreboding spruces were prophetic of coming storm. The season was summer, but the sparkle was gone. Everything conveyed some subtle suggestion of the severer season so lately past, so soon to come again. In the north country summer is but an armistice. Spirits run high, but there always remains the shadow of struggle, but scantily veiled. The pines have been too long wracked by winter winds to lose their sternness in a short six weeks or the spruces their hint of snow. Spring's pennants proclaim that the truce is on; but an August frost is like to slay in treachery. It is a long defense that trees and animal and man have to make against the cold. But it breeds greatness.

The last carry, the last rearrangement in the canoe, and then the last five miles. Darkness had shut in, but the rain yet forbore. We remembered the exultation in our flight down that same channel only four days before. It might have been four weeks. Another mood had taken its place. We were pretty tired, but we were finishing strong; we were coming home. We had seen much and lived a good deal, and a cozy camp was awaiting us. Exultation might have passed, but satisfaction had come. There is something very bed-rock about satisfaction.

Around the cape decorated by the Carnegie establishment, and our strokes strengthened. We saw a fire. It was the Scouts'. They, then, were still hopeful. We paddled. They had been more than hopeful, faithful. They had a supper all prepared. It was downright religious of them. And it warmed our hearts that Luggins was so pleased to see us. Truly this was a home-coming. That night we slept the sleep of perfect harmony with life.

CHAPTER VII

UNCONSIDERED CRANBERRY

THE next day, with a northeast storm beating steadily down the lake, we lay in a glory of indolence within our castle. The rain had begun late in the night. I had heard the first slow and measured drops, half aroused, and had turned over in that most perfect luxury of warmth and weariness, drowsing away into the limbo of no more duties to do.

Every so often in camp you loaf and mend your outfit; every so often a rest is enforced by the weather. When these two conditions are coincident, delicious is the savor thereof.

It was a magnificent storm. A long roar pervaded the forest. But as our own position was sheltered we banished a fatuous sympathy for Luggins and set about enjoying it. Enjoying a nor'easter implies a lot of firewood, but we had that and could concentrate on maintaining a superior fire. At odd times we studied the map. The rain laid by in time to let us indulge in a supper of proportions, and in the afterglow of exaggerated kindliness, I broached a scheme that I had always longed to try.

The scheme was simple. It proposed to set our faces in a certain direction through the wilderness and, with no advice except that of the compass, to follow along until we had won our objective. In other words, I suggested that we play Daniel Boone.

I was able to go at once into particulars as to the direction. I asked Lynn the name of the biggest lake in the Adirondacks. He did n't know. I asked him in what section more bears were shot than in all others together. He could n't guess. I asked him if he 'd ever heard of Cranberry. He had n't.

Lynn was not the first person that I 'd stumped. In fact, for weeks before deciding where to strike into the Adirondacks, I had asked people about the Cranberry Lake section. I had never found one eye-witness. There were scores who had never heard of its existence. There were dozens who knew Keene Valley or the Saranacs or the Schroon Lake country, but had only heard vaguely of this western body of water. Several asked me to drop them a line about it when I should have visited it. Doubtless if I had made my inquiries in Buffalo or Utica or Carthage, I should have found some one whose grandson or second cousin had been near the spot.

ROADHOUSE OF THE OLD STAGING DAYS

Photo by New York State Conservation Commission

UNCONSIDERED CRANBERRY 147

Here, I thought, in considerable elation, is new ground. But before that evening I said nothing about it to Lynn. I had saved this most delectable news until the most inciting strategic moment. The effect was proper. The boy was infected with the subtle poison of exploration. We proposed to give the western Adirondacks to the world. "Cranberry or combust" became our cry.

Though the railroads would not have you think so, there is really no geography to enjoyment. The amount of gratification one gets varies not with the length of the green ticket, but with the strength of your imagination. I have always fixed the region vaguely adjacent to Hudson's Bay as the land where the nearest superior brand of adventure is to be had. But I doubtless could be just as uncomfortable nearer home. Miling away the time is a habit. It was begun by Marco Polo and encouraged by advertisement agencies. These agencies beg of you to see all of America first. They feature Niagara and Nitnit, Oregon, because it is so expensive to get there. They neglect Cranberry for the reverse reason and so does everybody else. I imagine that a thousand Americans have been to Sitka or up the Nile for every one who has toured the Adirondack plateau. This is a tribute, not to Sitka, but to the agencies.

The Adirondack plateau comprises the western third of the Park. Its level is between fifteen hundred and two thousand feet above sea. It is filled with little ponds and little mountains and little else. You can travel across great areas of second growth forest or better without seeing a farm. It furnishes a breeding ground for game, second only to the well-watched estates for deer, and second to no other place for bear and the small fur animals. The fishing varies, but chiefly among the superlatives. The scenery does not. It never takes your breath unless you 're easily winded. It was into country such as this, recommended by none, yet so near to all, that our curiosity was to lead us.

The northeast storm blew itself out during the night, but left a drizzle to blot out an unambitious landscape, which it did effectively for two more days. We used these, however, in perfecting our readiness and storing energy for the attack. Even Luggins, I risk believing, was ready for a change, even though it involved motion.

Consequently we were all joyful the next morning when the sun shone upon an amphibious world. By a supernal show of self-control we gave but half an hour to Brandreth trout and had our lunch well along the shore of North Pond. "Tomorrow," we said, "we will be in uncharted waters." Cranberry lay northwest by north, and with a sense of exhilaration, we left the road and plunged toward it.

It was pleasant walking in the wood. The trees were tall, the undergrowth inconsequential, and Lynn, who was a master-packer, had tied Luggins most engagingly to his load. There is nothing quite so hard to do as stacking bread, bedding, and the rest of a camper's miscellany upon a horse, and binding it there to stay. There is no art so discouraging to the amateur. It is awkward learning to swim, and to master the violin is a saddening business. But to arrange things on a horse's back tests one's nature. Arrange, heave, tie as you will, unless you have the skill of the chosen, the items of your load will fall passionately to earth. There is no beginner's luck in packing. The most you can hope for is that your beast does not run off when the furniture slips beneath his belly. Lynn, however, had learned his lesson in Wyoming, and we made progress through the open forest without mishap.

Our camp was pitched beside Lake Lila, in Nehasane Park, Dr. Webb's purchase, now belonging, I believe, to an association which can be justly proud of its hundred thousand acres. At evensong we heard the rumble of the Montreal express. "To-morrow," we said, "we shall hear no train."

At ten of a beautiful morning we crossed the rails. The shining pathway curved, graceful and significant. As Luggins climbed the embankment, stepped gingerly across the steel, and paused, the contrast had almost the vividness of poetry. Our little caravan, recently so important and again to be so important to us, was all at once reduced to its proper proportions by contact with modern power. Our pleasures seemed small, our efforts infantile. To creep off into the woods, to set our hearts upon trout an inch longer than their fellows, to play house with a bit of waterproofing—these things in the stern sight of those rails seemed to discount ambition and render us open to just blame.

For one depressing moment the rails seemed to have the final word. Then from a little way within the wood came the song of the whitethroat, just once, but a solace to my feeling. It came not so robust now as in the springtime, but still rounded and crystal clear. "Ah! wonderful, wonderful, wonderful," was all, in descending revery, but singing in one's brain through the after-silence, was not pathos, but the earnestness of beauty in simplest song. It was a sufficient answer to the rails. We pushed on.

I would not like to rise in camp-meeting when it is time for the superstitious to go forward. But one does notice that three is the popular number for mishaps. Our sequence of misfortune began almost immediately after lunch. An animated southwest breeze was blowing. I was washing the dishes by a pond; Lynn was attending to

Luggins's lunch. A little pack-basket was bowled over and rolled into the fire. It was rescued before it had been much damaged, but our precious map was cindered. We were now in condition to play Daniel Boone in earnest. The railroad lay but an hour behind us, but we were unwilling to accept its haughty terms of security. We declined a separate peace with the wilderness.

One thing that we had over Daniel was a destination; even a direction. We were sure to hit Cranberry on one of its hundred and sixty-five miles of coast-line if we but kept long enough on our northwesterly course. The thing was not to hit anything else.

Our apparent indifference to calamity was shaken somewhat by our arrival near twilight upon the shores of a disconcerting bayou. It was elongated beyond sight, yet narrow enough to put the shot over. We rested, like Cæsar, to get a frog's-eye view (Lynn's description) of the swampy crossing. Trees did not grow quite close enough to fell a bridge-way. "And so," said Lynn, "school-boys will never have to read your classic account of that, at least." Luggins could swim, but we did not want to drown the duffle. To go around appeared an interminable task as the lay of land promised swamp. We prepared to camp, since dusk was at hand, although the situation was not perfection.

Then came the third disaster. We discovered that we had left our mosquito bar at Raquette, and that this was going to be a night foreordained for mosquito bar. The rank grass was a sort of sanatorium for the lyric insect, and this was its Saturday night. Luggins was already showing signs of nervousness. Slightly out of temper on account of our enforced encampment by a mere morass, we grew silent. I grew specially silent, because it was I who, in a spasm of preparation for the trip, had insisted upon washing out the mosquito bar and had left it soaking in a natural wash-basin. But the mosquitos made up for any silence on our part.

The mosquitos in the Adirondacks are not so numerous as on the northern plains, nor so robust as in the swamps of uncleared Jersey. But at times they can be enraging beyond the invention of words. In another chapter I must have my say, for it is a thing no writer of outdoors can resist. But being anxious to get to Cranberry, I shall here rest content with remarking that for choral harmonies and unity of purpose that was a red-letter night. It would have been difficult to have found a gathering busier or more distinguished. By building a vigorous smudge and mummifying ourselves in blankets, we escaped being torn limb from limb, but the uproar outside such a thin partition as a layer of wool was

UNCONSIDERED CRANBERRY

scarcely muffled. And when, at the coming of dawn, the pack began to realize that they had toiled all night and had taken nothing, their song rose into a cheerless and harrowing minor. It would have been less disturbing to have been quietly eaten. But fatigue had its way, and I was drowsing off when Lynn poked me in the ribs and asked me whether I thought that St. Paul had ever camped out or how had he got grounds for his pessimistic cry, "O death, where is *thy* sting!"

After our night of inaction any action took on an aspect of pleasantness. The traverse of the flow became an interesting problem. First we swam Luggins over, then bound together some logs with rope, and swam this raft over with the duffle on top, and as in the arithmetic problems, succeeded in transferring all the household gods in the smallest number of trips and the maximum of dryness. With a fervent but simple adieu we left this spot of unhallowed memory.

The day was without excitement, as was fitting. We followed a deer trail along the bank of a stream which had the goodness to favor our direction. It brought us to a fair and square body of water, covered with water-lilies and frogs. Our compass advised a turn to the right, but an emphatic little eminence forbade. We skirted this to the leftward and, coming upon a breezy natural clearing, decided to stop there for the night, far from the madding cloud. After putting our house in order, we decided that the little mountain would give us the lay of the morrow's land and climbed it. Unfortunately Adirondack hills do not rise to symmetrical and shiny apexes from which the landscape extends with geographical clearness on all sides. There is too much room at the top and it is mostly unherpicidal (Lynn's term). But we found a convenient tree from which we swayed and looked about us with that wild surmise that distinguished Balboa's travels. There was very little accurate information in the view. Arms of water appeared in various places to the westward. But the striking sight was the sea-like rolling of the landscape. Take the Bay of Biscay in a storm, magnify thirty diameters, and you reproduce this unfeatured wilderness in contour. Upholster it with trees and sprinkle with ponds and you complete the picture we had from our spruce-top. When we finally brought ourselves to the point of leaving, in the east the haze of twilight was beginning to rise, although Lynn insisted it was only a bank of mosquitos hovering over our last night's marsh. If being alone in the woods was our object, we had at last achieved it. The sky itself could not have been more vacant of habitation. We had reached a land where height and grandeur and the other qualities that are supposed to recommend mountains were lacking. But there was a

PHOTO BY WARWICK S. CARPENTER

INDIAN PASS BROOK; THE INFANT HUDSON

UNCONSIDERED CRANBERRY

charm about these little green cobs that coaxed one's interest and satisfied. Despise not the small topographies; it takes more than magnitude to make a mountain.

The weather had now settled down into a rut of pleasantness. We could go to sleep assured and awake unbetrayed. The morning brought us to a pond, the outlet of which, flowing to the northwest, we judged would bring us to Cranberry. On our right a long string of hills rose five or six hundred feet, and to the southwest there was another considerable rise. Early in the afternoon a broad sparkle ahead confirmed our suppositions. In ten minutes we had had our first swim in Cranberry.

Cranberry Lake, St. Lawrence County, is a favored sheet of water. Thanks to a dam, it has ranking place for size and length of shore-line. It is surrounded by forest. Hills rise from five to fifteen hundred feet above the lake level, itself fifteen hundred above the sea. Since the brooks are stocked with trout, and the woods are full of game, it is surprising that an enterprising lot of people should pass it by. There are two explanations. Until recently it has been very difficult to reach. The Grasse River lumber railroad from Childwold, which is the only direct route from the east, is but a three-year-old. Also the beauties of Cranberry are all of the quieter type. Compared to the dignities of the Marcy group, Cranberry mountains are beneath notice. Compared to the open vistas and connected waters of the lake systems of Hamilton and Franklin counties, Cranberry seems but a moody and isolated sister. And, even more prejudicial to its fame, was its beginning. The lumberers did not clear the shores that were to be flooded, and until recently the beauty of its shore-line was marred by dead trees. But time has ameliorated that. Exploration has put a hundred ponds upon the map— a hundred clear-water ponds that lie within six miles of the lake shores. The railroads will magnify the mountains, and the region will soon flow with milk (condensed) and money. Until the day, however, that the great public makes its discovery, the trapper will lay his traps, the fisherman cast his fly in the wildest section of the Adirondack Park. May the public rest in peace!

All of our information was ex post facto and very nearly post mortem, for I now have come to relate that which should not have to be related except of two youths who, lazy and swollen with good luck, threw caution to the winds. To say nothing of the waters!

But caution has never been a weakness of youth, and there were two extenuating circumstances. We had come out upon the lake at the end of a long arm. Since the best of my inquiries had never disclosed a person who had actually seen

UNCONSIDERED CRANBERRY 159

the lake and since those inquiries had been fairly general, it seemed fair to argue that the shores might be untenanted. Further, the season had already turned the Labor Day pivot after which home-seeking vacationists are happiest. Further still, I knew that there were a hundred and sixty-five miles of shore-line, so that it was quite mathematical to suppose that we might wander eighty-two and a half miles before we reached the village. Further still—but that was quite far enough. We decided to make a raft.

Two articles of civilization which stand pre-eminent on our lists of supplies are nails and rope. If Robinson Crusoe knew anything about camping beforehand, I'll wager that he saved nails and rope from his wreck before he began on the canned goods. We had enough of them. We also had enough wood and enough confidence in Luggins. So we firmly decided to make a raft.

Luggins, the obliging, was distinguished from all other quadrupeds by a guileless faith in humanity in general, and especially in Lynn. In the West I have seen Lynn lead him along places where angels would fear to tread. In fact, Lynn has the same faculty of leading or misleading the less dumb animals. In our nursery days when it was time to put away the playthings, Lynn could have the party working for him after union hours as one of the rarer privileges. So it is not surprising that an amiable horse should accede to his whims. I firmly believe that he could put a belt under Luggins's belly, buckle him to a balloon, and fly over the Rockies with him, and never a comment from the horse. Accordingly we anticipated no trouble on the raft. This we now finally decided to construct.

By nightfall we had built and floated the latest thing in boats, which we christened the "Aquatainia" for the same reason. It looked insubmarinable and impervious to storm. Our split-log platform took the place of boards, and our ground-cloth was substituted for the more formal sail. If the Cranberry-lakers did not shoot us on sight, we were sure of considerable glory. For once we did not dawdle over coffee in the morning.

Progress to the first point was slow. This gave Luggins opportunity to get his sea-legs on. His look was inscrutable. I never could decide whether, assuming that we were mad, he was committed to fate and should make the best of it, or whether never having lost his life, he was fearless merely from inexperience. The jerks of our poling and the quivering of the structure when the breeze began to flap the sail disturbed him not a whit. It was tolerant of him, I say.

Outside the sheltering point we were hurried at once into admiration of the lake and of the craft. Long stripling capes ran out into the water. Islands sat with graceful composure on the waves, and the even blue of the hills rose in the distance. The chug of a motor-boat came over the ripples. It pointed toward us. We were to be boarded by the curious. But much was to happen first.

We had by now progressed far enough from shore to expose ourselves to the freshening southwest wind. The force of this was sufficient to counteract all our efforts with the steering gear— a section of a sapling. At first gradually, but with increasing momentum our raft began to patronize a course that would bring us with mathematical exactness upon the rocky shores of an island. We endeavored to deviate. The sail drew us like destiny. We took it down. Luggins was a sail. We couldn't furl him. The island neared. The surf, fully a foot high, was dashing upon its stern and rockbound windward. The voyage was following the classic tradition. The aroma of shipwreck floated from the beach.

Finding that there was nothing to be done but wait the final shock, we bade Luggins be of good cheer and not give up the ship. At about three bells we struck, after which we led our fellow-adventurer off to enjoy the grass while we commenced to look for a sail, between cursory inspections of our isle. It was soon inspected. It covered an acre. It was a little further from the mainland than we cared to swim with the horse or his load. There were two courses to pursue. We must either attract the distant motor-boat or definitely decide to settle on the island.

From time to time many 's the person who has saved our lives (cooks leading), and their names have gone unrecorded. But friend Howland emerges from the wrack of the unidentified, for it was he in a brave little ship that lifted us from the maroon. He had distinguished the horse from afar in mid-voyage, had witnessed our casting away, and had brought his craft to our assistance. He had a laugh at our expense, but we had so many other commodities at his that the ledger has never tallied since. Thus did the manner of our coming to Cranberry differ from the coming of most.

With Mr. Howland to point out the polite interests of the place, and a dazzling sun to deck the wild, our ride up the flow to Wanakena was gladdening. Our host, tall, sunburned, robust, told us of bear-hunts and invited us to wait for the deer season. From his account the deer at Cranberry did not stand upon etiquette, but intruded upon the hunters. One had to shoot to get rid of their importunities. It sounded for excitement very like gunning in an orphan asylum; but in a locality where most of one's energy in winter is expended in keeping warm, I suppose that obtaining one's daily food does not need excitement. Howland said that he would show us game if we would go with him to the Plains. We agreed to show him how a horse could act in the woods if he would pilot us to a few congeries of deer on the Plains. We appointed Sunday for the exchange.

The Oswegatchie River is a complete demonstration of the art of curving. All the curves that Euclid knew and some that he dreamed about will be found on this river that runs around the hills. Howland had been used to slavishly following it in his canoe; Luggins opened his eyes to the art of annihilating space across country. When we got to the Plains there was n't a deer in sight. But we pitched the tent and busied ourselves about supper, and pretty soon the tawny ones began to appear like fireflies in a summer dusk. Exaggeration shall not figure in this chronicle: I believe we saw only seven, which Howland declared was "stingy little," but which we thought was very fair considering that the locality did not presume to be a zoo.

The Plains are crossed by a couple of roads, but their wide treelessness, surrounded by hospitable woods, gives them a distinction shared by few regions. The plateau just this side of the Cascade Lakes, the plains of Kenwells, the plains of the Oswegatchie always impress one. It is the contrast with the deep wood that makes them so refreshing.

On another day we paddled miles above the rapids on the Oswegatchie. The trout season had joined the snows of yesteryear which made it actual pain to float over places where little streams, entering from mossy coverts, guaranteed fish of reputation. In the near by and by we have planned a reunion with those fish.

We were told to visit Star Lake, of which everybody speaks well, but there was real exploration at hand. Back from the shores of Cranberry lie pools of unimaginable loveliness. To many run trails, but there are many others which even the deer do not frequent. We came upon three shut in by tall spruce, windless and dark as magic, tarns of such serenity that to come upon them seemed a violation.

With the fishing gone and the hunting not yet come, we were thrown upon the alternative of immediate further travel or of enjoying the lake as such. We could not leave it. The September days sharp in the morning and crisp at night had set all the colors flowing up the hills. Weeks before in August the swamp maples had flamed out. But now the tuning up was over, and the great symphony about to begin. Here and there whole sugar-maples shone from the green, and groves of beeches were starting into yellows and bronzes

Photo by Warwick S. Carpenter

HANGING SPEAR FALLS OF THE OPALESCENT

and golds. New variations of maroon sidled up to vermilions unabashed. The fulfilment was to come weeks later, so long and long is the autumn dream in these corridors of heaven. And to us this was almost the most beautiful part of it—the change from day to day so deliberate as to arrest belief in ultimate decay, so constant that each morning arrayed new panoramas of admiration.

Cranberry Lake is large enough to make a sailing canoe worth the rigging, and its shores are not so funneled by high mountains as to flaw the wind. We put side boards and an eight-foot mast in an eighteen-footer, and cruised like lotus-eaters.

Below the lake the Oswegatchie wanders around until it gets to a sixty-foot cascade. But Lynn and I decided that Buttermilk had been enough for us, and after one final ride about the lake with Mr. Howland, we set out from Cranberry Lake Village, eastward, along the line of the Grasse River Railroad for Childwold and points east.

We left the smiling expanses of Cranberry and its hospitable neighborhood with the compunctions of deserters. After Labor Day in the remoter Park the philosophy of welcome undergoes a change. During July and August a transient tide inundates the famous centers, covers the outlying districts thinly, and even trickles into the obscurest corners. The tide is chiefly of new and thoughtless foamy people with whom the inhabitants share their food and sometimes drink, but never their innermost thought. They live on the surface and in the pockets of these summerers. They serve obligingly, but also reserve much.

The winter inhabitant is another man. He sloughs off the characteristics of a corner grocery and buds with the qualifications of a comrade. He knows everything of the woods; he has done everything that strong hunters do, and he is willing to tell you about it. There is also plenty of time because, barring a few chores, his next engagement is in the spring. Of course the younger men have the wood-chopping and ice-getting and a little hunting on their calendars, but even for them there are many days when the sole if almost continuous duty is to feed sticks of white split wood into the stove.

The calendar of an Adirondack citizen reads remarkably like an index to a vacation guide. For example:

New Year's day; getting in the ice; sugaring off; the spring drive (pulp-wood); trout season opens; digging-the-garden season opens; baiting-the-boarder season opens; summer guiding; deer season passes; bear season begins; fire-wood; Xmas.

Nobody, I notice, has written a "Boy Scouts in the Adirondack" series; for authors, after all, have a regard for their reputations and the pleasures of the park are too incredible for fiction.

On the way out from Cranberry we met a good father, a Catholic sky-pilot who, instead of trying to convert Luggins to the Church, immediately plunged into a description of the best fishing-holes on Brandy Brook. This particular stream has received considerable homage in the literature of the country, for it seems to overflow with generous trout who are willing to sacrifice themselves at any time for the sake of a record catch. The Grasse River, along which we were expecting to travel, also presents opportunities for fish to broaden their lives, which, it is reported, they avariciously accept. Unfortunately, I cannot give either the confirmation or the lie to this rumor. We were both so perpetually under obligations to game wardens as well as to the wilderness, that we had no desire to poach. As Lynn said, it was only natural to desert your wife if she spoke unkindly to you, and a murder now and then relieved you from the stigma of pacifist, but no man with gratitude in his chest would catch trout under-size or out of season. The Commission maintains nine hatcheries which pour fry into the brooks all over the Park, rendering it possible for thousands of fishermen to partly furnish their dinner tables free, with a prince's hospitality. The man who slaughters small fish steals twice, once from himself and once from everybody else.

The trip along the railroad was scarcely a triumphal journey either for us or the Adirondacks. The sky-pilot, whose name I unworthily forget, cheered us with reminiscence and kindly gossip until he had to turn off toward a lumber camp, and we were warmer of heart for having been companions to him. The sight of this old man enduring what must have been considerable privation for age was fortifying to the sterner virtues, and I'll argue that he had some result from his impromptu sermonings in God's tabernacle.

Along this railroad, as I say, the Adirondacks are neither water, wood, nor mountain. Inconsequential hills rise, covered with a man-eaten forest, and through and between wander discouraging waterways which own up to being neither swamps nor streams. A lumber company of the first dimension has great private holdings hereabouts and is speedily exacting the uttermost of them. We walked between raw embankments cut for the recent railroad and at the end of the afternoon passed great brown plains on which deer were feeding. A few minutes brought us to Conifer, where a sawmill gormandizes night and day.

At Conifer we found an interesting group of men, as the directors of lumbering enterprises always are. The public estimation of a lumber-king is of a person who goes about surveying what he may devour at the expense of the people, the land, and the future. And the public has been too often right. But there is another side to the character —the growing side. Selfishness is becoming economy; indiscriminate destruction is becoming selective conscription; the effrontery of theft, at least dissimulation. Legislatures are not bribed so openly or in such a wholesale manner as heretofore; the eyes of the Commission are in every place. And some day—let us hope before all private holdings have been made a desert—scientific cutting will leave the woodland, not a forest fire trap, but a thing of beauty—and of dividends.

At Conifer the company maintains a good hotel, which is a thing to know. In winter the whole process can be watched to the most enjoyable advantage; the selected tree, the falling-place prepared, the sawing, and the fall, the trimming, and the cutting into logs, the skid-way to the train, the water, and endless chain, and the little door into the mill, through which enters the log that comes out board. The men working in the snow have the longest hours of any in our country—twelve, usually, with half an hour for dinner. But they do not seem to be a complaining or a striking set, probably dreading a sixteen-hour night more than they would relish an eight-hour day. They are men with a handsome muscle, not over-young, for a boy under thirty cannot stand the labor. He must be well set. Their food is good. The adventurous used to run away to sea, but not in the desperation of logic. And it would have been better for many of them if they had run to wood. The forest is austere, but it does not retaliate.

At Conifer the voice of the map was again heard. The summer had gone, and we had yet to see almost all the famous sections of the Adirondacks. So we eliminated Lake Massawepie from our consideration, and a further acquaintance with Big Tupper also, and after revictualing at the company's store we dived once more into the woods, intending to come out upon the paradise that made Paul Smith.

CHAPTER VIII

ANIMALS OF THE ADIRONDACKS

IT was annoying to find how blind we were. Every pond shore, every beech-grove, and tamarack swamp besought us to look and to look sharply. When we did look, we invariably saw something, but our eyes soon filmed again, and our conversation hazed off into space. You will find that it is much more difficult to discuss the visible than the invisible if you ever pause for a moment in your discussion of the wrongs of poverty to bandy technical terms about any feature of the marvelous machine which is the world. A spellbinder who finds sermons all too short for his remarks about our glorious immortality might be seriously stumped if asked to confine his reflections to the wild-flowers that adorn his pulpit.

I am beginning to believe that the speculative spiritualities can wait upon the spiritualities-at-hand. It seems almost as worthy a worship to sing, "I admire and praise thee, O winter wren," as to sing, "I admire and praise thee, O God," because the chances are that you are more intelligently sincere. If this is exaggeration, it is necessary to emphasize the fact that our physical and spiritual eyes function such a small part of their possibilities. For, leaving out the worship, to SEE nature requires more eyesight than is usually expended. Read Muir, Audubon, Thoreau, and Burroughs, and realize how much of every day is left unseen. When Lynn and I found out by some unusual spasms of attention how much of the main spectacle we were missing, we set ourselves to seeing. It annoyed us to find how blind we had been.

One of the best tests for blindness that any one could devise would be a week or, better yet, a month in the North Woods. There are a hundred kinds of birds there in the spring and forty sorts of mammals the year round, yet how many does the average tourist see? During the first two weeks of our trip Lynn and I saw a chipmunk, a squirrel, and a mosquito. We knew there were deer, and we heard the frogs. If it hadn't been for some extremely interesting noises and some tracks, we might never have wakened up. As Lynn very properly put it, it was we who were extinct.

But down in the Cedar River country, where it is wild enough for anything to happen, we thought we heard a panther. We were sure we saw a wildcat. These amateur beginnings were responsible for some later study. We got out the books. We

Photo by Warwick S. Carpenter

SOUTH FROM THE SUMMIT OF INDIAN PASS

followed tracks till our noses began to point. We set night cameras and talked with old guides and trappers. From them, chiefly, and from Merriam, this chapter issues, and not from our pitiful observations only, as I wish it could. Dr. Clinton Hart Merriam in his rides and hunts among the mountains saw thirty-nine kinds of mammals, and if a man keeps his eye open, he may do nearly as well. We thought that we did well to increase our four to twenty-four. The list of possibilities follows, for hunting, even with a pencil and check-list, is still the royal sport.

There are three quadrupeds that prey upon the imagination—three that gentlemen of the wild long to have encountered or to have seen: the wolf, the panther, and the wildcat.

The thirst for wolves is the fault of fairy tales, I suppose. To lay a foundation for veracity at the outset, I must say that we saw none. The wolf is definitely gone from the Adirondacks. The last one, old and yellow-fanged, was killed near Brandreth the year of the Chicago Exposition. The deer of the Park are forever safe from them. But during the boyhood of many living guides, they were a pest. One howler would sound like a pack; a pack of six like perdition. They stole venison from camps; they destroyed great numbers of deer, helpless in the snow. It took large quantities of hares, frogs, mice, and skunk to maintain them in their gauntness. But they are gone, and great romance somehow perishes with them.

The panther, too, is almost certainly among the missing. I would like to be corrected, to be told (with proof) that in the fastness of the western plateau or on the ridges of the high east panthers still scarred the flanks of deer which in their decadence they missed. But it is a forlorn hope. Even the panther is a trifle moth-eaten and forlorn when looked at in the scientific glare. He is a coward; he does not lurk on horizontal branches of big trees to fall upon his paralyzed victims; he does not even make night hideous for belated travelers or twilight children by blood-curdling yells. He leaves that to the loons or the owls or the rarebits in which the raconteur has been indulging. And even if he had slain somebody, he wouldn't sling him over his shoulder and start for his lair. He would drag him to a fallen spruce or other covert and eat him up bit by bit, a child lasting, I presume, about two days, a deer nearly a week. The panther remains in the neighborhood till that particular ration is finished. Otherwise there would have been no catching him, for he can travel thirty miles a day. Some of the leaps that the panther made, measured in the snow, were enormous. On one occasion he covered forty feet on the third bound toward a deer, and on the record jump, which was from a twenty-foot ledge, he sprang sixty feet, knocking his prey a rod. It is the men who have shot panthers and have lived where they abounded who assert that panthers do not yell. Unfortunately this is at variance with good fiction. Bounty was paid on forty-six panthers in the Adirondacks in the ten years following 1871. As yet I have been able to get no information as to a single child or man having been carried off by the tawny cat, but I still have hopes.

There are two lynxes, the Canadian loup-cervier, and the ordinary wildcat of the story for boys. The Canadian lynx rarely comes as far south as the park, and the wildcat finds the climate too severe or else the supply of barnyard fowl too scarce. The lynx haunts the deep forest, while the wildcat is satisfied with the wood-lot if it be a good-sized one. Whatever it was that Lynn and I heard, it was probably neither.

During the fifties moose were shot in the northwest Adirondacks, the last recorded killing being in 1861. The moose is another animal that will probably never again thrive in these mountains because it demands large range. Their food is lily-pads, browse, and bark, and the nearness of men worries them as it does not at all the deer.

But there are two large animals that are numerous, and a third that promises to be: the deer, the black bear, and the elk. This last was an old resident. Occasional horns of the elk have been unearthed, and in the thirties hunters were still taking shots at the living elk. Recently elk brought from Wyoming have been liberated and are reported as increasing. There is no reason why the excess wintering in Jackson's Hole should not be brought in numbers to their old habitat.

The bear in the Adirondack Park is not nearly so decorative as in the Yellowstone, where he can be seen indulging his predatory instincts upon empty prune cans. Once a cub ran across the road almost under Luggins's nose. But while Lynn and I came upon bear sign and bear robes, and captured bear cubs, and even bear tracks in our Adirondack wanderings, we never yet have seen the bruin. But many a better hunter hasn't either. The surest way is to set out deliberately with either spade or gun for him. He homes in the most recessful forests, and his hearing is so acute that a mere stalker has not a tenth the chance that he has with the deer.

To the guns of the old guides many a fat bear has fallen. Just last autumn LeGrand Hale of Keene Valley killed one so large and so fat that he could pull the fat off in layers. When tried out, it filled several gallon jars. And in the wilderness about Cranberry Lake dozens of bears are killed every year. There is a great difference of opinion as to the palatability of bear-meat, which itself varies considerably with the age and season.

I have always wanted to find a bear's holing-up place. They tell me that these dens vary in elaborateness, from an impromptu shelter under a fallen spruce to an excavation in a hill lined with moss, depending upon the expected severity of the winter. It is my contention that bears, with the rest of the animal tribe, can have only the dimmest apprehension of atmospheric states to come, and it is easier to believe that a bear is driven to shelter only by the failure of the food supply or the actual deepening of the snow covering. Hibernation is merely nature's economy, the prolonging and intensifying of our own sleep to offset the high cost of hunting nuts.

A bear's menu is varied and continuous, I should judge, for how else can a half ton to a ton of meat be kept warm? It would read:

Ant eggs and the ants

Berries on and with the bush

Fish   Frogs   Turtles

Poultry

Pig, sheep, calf

Vegetables   Cherries

The Bee, the honey, and the honeycomb

Sweet apples

Mice   Acorns   Crickets   Grapes

It would be discouraging for mere man to collect a meal like that from a not too productive wilderness. Pity the poor bear!

Lynn and I were assured in several quarters that bears would never molest a man unless the young were threatened. There is no animal in the Adirondack Park that does not obey the same ruling. I only wish it were as true of the insects.

There is only one species of bear found in the Park and that is the black. It must take a good many females lurking in the fastnesses to perpetuate the race. Each mother brings forth two or, at most, three cubs at intervals of two or three years. These are so very infantile, being as small as squirrels when born, and requiring forty days for their eyes to open, that the animal deserves the highest tribute for exercising the intelligence to escape extermination.

The Conservation Commission through its game-wardens, reports that the deer of the Adirondacks roam about in greater numbers than ever before. There are good reasons for this. The Indian no longer has his autumn drive; the wolf and the panther do not decimate them in the snow; the game hog can no longer fatten upon his slaughterings unpenalized. The feeling among lumberjacks has perceptibly changed; and soon the settler, even if he were unwatched, would hesitate to kill more than his need because of the growing sentiment for conservation. The result is financial gain. Thousands of sportsmen, whose license fees and patronage have transformed the status of the inhabitant, kill their thousands of deer. But the laws are so wisely written and so well observed that the wilderness, instead of being a shot-out region, fairly struts with does and is well peppered with bucks. In every Garden of Eden there is the fool, but while he still strews bean-cans about, still leaves his camp-fire smoldering, he is learning to look for horns and not to shoot at the first bit of khaki that he sees. The fool learns only by compulsion, as the poacher by prison bars. We owe it to the splendid supervision by the Commission that the Park is anything but a treeless, gameless expanse of melancholy.

During our peregrinations we saw deer in almost every conceivable circumstance: standing rump-high in water, jumping twelve-foot bushes, descending precipitous, rocky banks that demanded caution at every step, standing at attention, running beside a fawn, swimming, waist-deep in snow, sizzling in strips over October coals. But I have never seen one asleep, although they probably indulge. Once we pitched our tent by a runway, and the first night we were aware of passing inquisitors. Once we made a salt-lick near a permanent camp—this is a highly illegal thing to do, we afterwards found, even for photographic purposes—and within ten days the ground was stamped as bare as a barn-yard, the salt-impregnated trunks licked bare of bark.

The chief surprise to me is always the length of the deer's tail. When held over its back, as in flight, it wig-wags truce in capitals.

Deer eat, I believe, about everything that grows from Mother Earth; lily-pads and berries in summer, nuts in the fall, and twigs and lichens in the winter. During summer it takes only half an eye to discover the creatures along the water-courses of a morning or evening, but after the beeches start to change, they gradually mount the ridges. In the severest weather they again come down to the frozen lakes and subsist on the thick fringe of trees at the margins. I used to believe that the deer-yards one reads about in boy-hunter stories were carefully trampled enclosures, surrounded by rows of lynx and catamounts grinning hungrily upon the herd huddled in the geometrical center. Deer-yards are more nearly trails formed by the restless browsings of the ill-fed animals. They stay in one locality till the browse is gone. You can easily see where they have slept.

The Virginia deer, which weighs about two hundred and fifty pounds in the Adirondacks, two hundred in Virginia, and one hundred and fifty in Florida, has an excessively busy time of it in changing his appearance. As a fawn, he is

Photo by the New York State Conservation Commission

MIDSUMMER MILDNESS

spotted for three or four months—the most beautiful little thing in the world. As an adult, he grows antlers for three months, rubs the velvet off, and then sheds them in about four more. Meanwhile his coat changes from reddish in the summer to bluish in the winter. The bucks become bull-necked and obstreperous in the rutting season, November. The does usually have two fawns.

I have heard of no instances where man has tried poison upon the deer, but every other means has been taken to rid the Park of this malicious animal. If you have an ounce of sportsman blood (but only one) in your body, you wait till March snows accumulate to the height of the deer and a crust forms. This the deer breaks through, but you, on snow-shoes, do not. Then you run alongside the ferocious and big-eyed doe until its heart breaks, and you can take it safely. Another, less fatiguing method, is to make a salt-lick and snipe at the beasts. Another is to unleash some dogs, pick out a comfortable spot, and wait until they drive the deer into the lake. This is tedious, but sure, as the only way the deer can shake the dogs is to take to water, and the hunter can then butcher her at his pleasure. A fourth method necessitates sitting in a boat for an hour or more while your fellow sportsmen paddle you around, the boat being screened from the deer's sight by the glare from a jack-lantern or sheltered torch. When the brute of a deer stands inquisitive and lovely, you shoot her down at close range.

But all this has been changed by law. Instead of does as well as bucks being killed in or out of season by these lazy and unsportsmanlike methods, now only bucks with horns can be secured and then only within well-defined seasons by the one self-respecting mode of hunting, called still-hunting. In this game you carry your own gun, stalk through the forest in daylight, and endeavor to see farther and hear quicker than this most gifted animal. If you can trail him to his thicket, keep always down the wind from him, and at the end refrain from shooting if his head is not to your fancy; then you are a huntsman who deserves the name.

One of the greatest excitements of our trip was caused by our first beaver-dam. We had not known that the beaver had returned to the Adirondacks. We came upon the dam in deep woods while we were making a short cut above Speculator and fancied callowly enough that a discovery was about to be launched among admiring naturalists. Even when some profane reflections upon beaver had been delivered to us by a Park farmer, our satisfaction was only slightly watered. But when, in after-weeks, we were forced to long detours or parlous wadings, our interest in this devilishly industrious beast changed and waned

ANIMALS OF THE ADIRONDACKS 189

until we fell into active sympathy with the irate farmer. There is no doubt that in some parts of the Park the beaver has become a pest.

It is possible that the race of beavers never completely died away. But even in the thirties they were rarer than wolves in the eighties. One was caught in 1837, one in 1841, one in 1880 in the Raquette. A few years ago a pair were liberated and protected, and as each mother bears four a year, and as the country was full of their chief food, the poplar, the family spread like Noah's after the flood. Already a few have had to be removed by the Commission in the Fulton Chain region and in a few years more there can very easily be allowed a short open season. It is no wonder that the Iroquois called this region the Beaver Hunting Country. The New Netherlands, according to the eye-witness, Adriaen van der Donk, furnished eighty thousand skins a year. There was some excuse for beaver hats being the style.

It is an amazing and elusive creature, this flat-tailed rattish-looking gnawer. His dam is comprehensible, his house possible, but the size of the trees he cuts down, the science of the felling, the laborious chopping into size, the carting to the pond—these things astound one. The dams come any size. They are packed hard by industry and the stream's current, and upon them you may find the foot-prints of other animals. They often form a highway across a swamp. The house is an apartment house, with sometimes as many as four families on the two floors. It is storehouse, shelter, school-house, and dormitory. When actual winter commences, it freezes as hard as cement and must smell like a tenement.

The beaver's food is chiefly poplar, birch, and alder bark with leaves. The cut trees always fall toward the pond. The beaver's tooth must be the hardest in nature to withstand the perpetual chiseling. I have seen birches nine inches across that had been felled by the sweat of their jaws.

Dusk and dawn are the only times to see the beaver at work, and that requires the utmost patience and secrecy. Twice we came upon the head of a beaver swimming slowly up-stream, and each time did he duck without that romantic sentinel shot from the flat of his tail. But such alarms are not fiction. There has, however, been plenty of fiction written about this most unobserved animal, Pliny perpetrating the worst. When Mr. Leacock wishes inspiration for more nonsense novels, he can easily score another bull's-eye by shooting at the broad absurdities of the ancient and denatured naturalists.

There is one animal in the Adirondacks that the blindest, be he unable to distinguish between a chipmunk and a red squirrel, cannot miss. He makes a track like a little old baboon, bear-wise; he chatters at night, conversationally if pleased, and angrily if disturbed. He weighs about fifteen pounds, advances sluggishly toward you, but retreats at a good pace if you chase him. He will sell his spines for salt. And now you know for certain what you had already guessed.

Whether it was the salt that we kept for Luggins, or just because we were easy marks and they knew it, I cannot tell. But Lynn and I certainly put up with a plague o' porcupines. At first we shooed them away and then we killed them. Their choicest hour was two A. M. This is unusual, for most animals, popular opinion to the contrary, are not mid-nocturnal, but fonder of the dimness before dawn and after sunset. Two A. M. to an accompaniment of rattled pans is an aggravation that we discouraged with axes, with a gun, with fires. But still came the porkies, and still we buried them intact, until we were admonished to try their livers. Do it yourself; they are delicious.

There is no earthly reason why porcs of the wild wood should not make delicious eating, if properly treated. Their food is hemlock bark and the ends of birch and maple branches. They will strip a hemlock before leaving it. One is easily passed by for a crow's nest lodged in some dim crotch. Indeed, his only enemies are man and the big owls, and I fail to see how they can make much of him.

Much armament has made the porcupine stupid. One night I heard one in our tent, scared him up a tree, and being too lazy to get him then, tied a bath towel around the trunk and threw an extra log on the fire. The silly beast stayed up in the tree all night. Why they always began operations on the aluminum pans was something that I never could guess. They were less salty than other things and always woke us. We dreaded a chase in the dark, but still more we dreaded to kill one in the tent, for it meant avenues of quills to be dis-encountered for days after.

Some of the quills on the larger 'pines are two inches long, of a beautiful black-and-whiteness and savagely barbed. They will work through anything, but an armor-clad, because they will go only one way and muscular action impels them. They cause inflammation, but not death to animals. It is not unusual to find quills imbedded in their flesh. The tail is capable of filling your hand or your dog or your shoe with a score of quills, each one of which is a separate torture to remove. If you add to his munition factory, his disagreeable odor, his ability and ambition to gnaw down your house, his abominable perseverance, you have a sufficient reason to abjure him. But he is so unusual that it would be a pity not to have him at least represented in the big woods. There is plenty of room. I have never seen the little ones, but they must make cute little pincushions.

While discussing black and white, one cannot pass by the skunk. The black of him is particularly handsome, and when the rare one, lacking the white stripe, is found, it is probably sold for something else. It is a matter for pity that the beast is not formed on more graceful lines, as we have the evidence of all skunk-farmers and some photographs of Mr. Ernest Thompson Seton's to show that they make gentle and cleanly pets. Dr. Merriam kept ten such pets, and they liked to be caressed and never tried to bite, not to mention offering more painful familiarities. It is possible to remove the scent bags without injuring the animal, a precautionary measure, for if too suddenly approached or accidentally injured, they have been known to assume the offensive.

Like porcupines, skunks have grown careless of danger because of danger's regard for their defense. They walk abroad, slowly and brazenly, at dusk and dawn, and it is for pedestrians to get out of their way. Sometimes automobiles cannot do this in time.

Although vast numbers are taken for their skins, the skunk persists, thanks to the eight or ten skunklets that infest the home each spring. It must be presumed that a rather strict discipline prevails within the hole.

Dr. Merriam, having eaten the flesh of skunk, cooked in every style, asserts that it "is white, tender, sweet, and is delicious eating. It is not unlike chicken, but is more delicate, and its taste is particularly agreeable." Chickens feed upon bugs and worms, so there is no reason, I suppose, to be squeamish about skunk, whose food is chiefly grasshoppers, frogs, bird's eggs, beetles, and other insects. Objectors please reflect upon the source of their breakfast bacon.

Dr. Merriam's dissection of the animal's defense is very interesting:

> His chief weapon lies in the secretion of a pair of anal glands that lie on either side of the rectum and are imbedded in a dense gizard-like mass of muscle, which serves to compress them so forcibly that the contained fluid may be ejected to the distance of 4 or 5 meters (13 to 16½ feet). Each sac is furnished with a single duct that leads into a prominent nipple-like papilla that is capable of being protruded from the anus and by which the direction of the jet is governed.

Dr. Wiley of Block Island "distinctly perceived the smell of a skunk, although the nearest land was twenty miles distant."

A skunk cannot be killed by a rifle-ball through the heart, or by the cleanest stroke of an ax, without discharging its scent. But if its back is broken by a sharp blow, not a drop will be emitted. The

Photo by the New York State Conservation Commission

THE FIRST REINFORCED CONCRETE

spinal cord's fracture is the only way to preserve skin and meat. Contrary to popular belief, a skunk, even in a trap, may be safely approached if he is not excited or hurt.

In our forest travels Lynn and I came upon very few skunks, and we never tried even the most unexcitable approaches upon them. As the black and white beauty lives chiefly upon meadow-products, he is as scarce as many a wilder animal in the deep woods. But like his unique and spiny neighbor, I hope that he will continue to inhabit them in reasonable numbers.

Whatever may have happened to all the other kinds of foxes that once denned in the wilderness, the ordinary red fox is the only one that is to be seen now, I believe. And his bark is more noticed than his brush. Like the skunk, he frequents the edges of the wilderness in greater numbers than the interior, because chickens are more easily caught than squirrels, and field-mice are more numerous than their woodland brothers. Next to the bear there is no animal whose tastes are so catholic; fish, muskrats, eggs, even young lambs, and strawberries make equally acceptable fox food. And Æsop's choice of grapes was not the fabulous part of the fable.

The fox's curiosity is matched only by his cunning or he would not survive. Time and again we found his tracks in the snow, wandering out of the wood, following some lumberman's or hunter's trail for a mile and then, his own satisfaction having been attained, disappearing. In our summer camps we heard him bark on the shores of many a pond. Once right around from our tent in a cove a fox stood on the shore and barked at some young sheldrakes, feeding out of reach, whether from disappointment or mere puppy fun we could not determine.

It is far easier to find a fox's burrow than a bear's, but one actually meets with more bear cubs on exhibition than the more lovely and beautiful offspring of Reynard. Unfortunately young foxes soon begin to practise treachery and other Punic virtues. But they are marvelously beautiful in their tawny and white shapeliness. It is a pity that the too vivacious as well as the too good should have to die young.

Still rarer in the greenwood and even commoner on its outskirts, is the always-old-gentleman woodchuck. From a broad meadow as many as thirty can be trapped in a summer, and yet the supply never totally fails. A pair usually have four or six young a year.

Despite his distaste for the pathless and cloverless woods, Lynn and I came upon a hermit of a 'chuck who had made his burrow under the sill of a guide's cabin twenty-two miles from the nearest field. It was in August, and Arctomys (as we called him after his scientific surname) came out only in the hottest hours of the afternoon. What he fed upon, we never could determine. The guide had a little garden. The deer jumped the fence and ate the lettuce, but we never discovered as much as one print of Arctomys' plantigrade paw in it. He probably ate the potato tops after the skunks and porcupine had finished eating the bugs.

'Tomys appeared as intelligent as Alice's dormouse. He never formed an opinion about us in the three days we were there, always disappearing into his hole when we moved, always coming up in thirty seconds to see if we would move again. One rainy morning we set about dishousing 'Tom', but after digging under difficult circumstances for about twenty feet, Lynn said it wasn't a house but a subway, and we decided to leave natural history to the naturalists.

The woodchuck is a puzzle. How does an inert, undefended creature survive? Even his habits are unintellectual. He begins to dorm at the autumnal equinox when the fields are full of feed; he wakes at the spring solstice when green grass is four weeks off and two feet under snow. He can climb trees only with a rush; he does not drink water; the most he can do to scare you is to whistle; he under-burrows whole fields and chuckles, as Mr. Corning remarks, "to see a mowing-machine, man and all, slump into one of these holes and disappear." He is excellent chicken food when hashed fine and boiled. And yet it is the woodchuck and not the wolf that inherits the earth.

In the interior the raccoon is even rarer, though by journeying from clearing to clearing, these wanderers do get to most parts of the wilderness. His monkey abilities and foxy cunning avail him nothing if one sets out deliberately to get him. He will not run far before treeing and will always investigate corn on the ear, no matter how obvious the trap. His black-and-gray handsomeness varies much with the individual animal.

The coon spends his days in solitude, high up in the hollow of some tree, but joins the family at night. Lynn and I had no chance to try the flesh of young coons, which is supposed to be pretty good. The two we found were very elderly.

For the man who is not properly located for beaver, the muskrat forms an entertaining substitute, and for all the commonness of the creature, there is a surprisingly widespread ignorance of his ways. On most ponds and every sluggish stream his trails, burrows, houses, or depredations will be found. Although he is the most trapped animal of our country, he persists partly because of a certain cunning and partly because it is not unknown for one couple to furnish a score or more of ratlets to the general horde each season.

ANIMALS OF THE ADIRONDACKS

Muskrats are busiest at night, and any time that you are out for deer, you will be startled by the splash a self-launched muskrat makes. It is easier far to surprise them in the daytime than to stalk a beaver, but none the less a test of woodsmanship.

A muskrat builds a house, not by careful masonry, as does the beaver, but by throwing together as much water-plant roots and grass as he thinks he will eat during the winter and then residing in it. There are certain conveniences to life in the pantry, but certain inconveniences about devouring your shelter at the most unseasonable time of year. I never observed any particular storing of food inside, but Dr. Merriam says that in the north it is done.

The easiest way to trap muskrats is to mine their trails, but their huts can be attacked in several ways. The skins are worth very few cents apiece, despite the fact that in one year half a million were sent to England.

Luggins' road and ours was being continually enlivened by a lot of little animals, the common rabbit, an occasional and most startling hare, the friendly chipmunk, and the vociferous red squirrel. Our camps were visited by mice—wood-mice, field-mice, house-mice, and, most charming of all, the long-tailed, white-footed mouse.

The childlike notion of valuing creation on account of size has waylaid us all. It is hard to consider a mouse as interesting as a moose. The white-footed is in reality far more beautiful than any moose, just as the magnolia warbler is more beautiful than a buzzard, cinquefoil than sun-flowers, contentment than the most ravishing display. But it takes observation and reflection to make sure, and only after Lynn and I had set ourselves to seeing things instead of skipping from spectacle to spectacle, did we begin to enjoy the peculiar delights of the sights we had always missed. There were many mammals that persisted beyond the fringe of our vision—the shrews, moles, bats, flying squirrels. And there remained obdurately hidden the prowlers of the dusk, which we caught unsatisfactory glimpses of and which we traced in morning light, the fierce inhabitants of forests that made for them the most perfect home.

The number of mink, otter, marten, and weasels that are concealed by Adirondack wilderness cover would probably astonish the trappers, and would certainly be a revelation to most tourists, who are not aware that such creatures are living in their midst. I shall never forget my astonishment at seeing a weasel chase a mouse about the corners of one of our camps or the interest of our first otter or the excitement of the young minks. These fairly common animals were not even known to me by name, at least as creatures that might cross our path, and the study of this submerged circle of nature was more thrilling than scrutiny of our better acquaintances.

The little weasel is very small, and mice and moles are its chief victims, but the stoat, the white weasel of winter, with a long and wiry body, does not stop at huge rats. It is credited with being the blood-thirstiest creature alive, killing for the fun of it long after its hunger is satisfied. It eats only the blood and brains of the chickens, squirrels, and rabbits. Its beady eyes and cruel snout are rather terrifying to a human from their inhuman suggestiveness of rapacity.

We had some good views of a mother mink and her four young that came out of their burrow at twilight and sometimes in broad afternoon and played about like cats. I never saw the mother bring any food, but we watched patiently enough to see her catch the fish that naturalists describe as her chief diet.

The sport that we were most anxious to see was an otter sliding, for we found their tracks and what we thought was their slide, but we never found the animal in conjunction with his mud bank. Otter swim so well and will go under water for such distances that it is almost impossible to get a good view of them till after snow has fallen. Their fur is the most valuable of any of the Park beasts. The last report from a member of the Commission stated that the number of otter, as of all the other fur-bearing animals, is increasing.

This, then, is the tale of wilderness inhabitants to-day. Nobody will see a wolf or a panther or a moose or a wolverine, let him be ever so wide awake. But his vigilance may be rewarded by a glimpse of a wildcat, an elk, mink, otter, or black bear. On the edge of the wood he will find raccoon, skunk, woodchuck, and the gray squirrel. Even if he is a careless goer, he cannot fail to startle a deer, surprise the porcupine, be scolded by the red squirrel, and scrutinized by the chipmunk. His evening camp will be visited by mice, while the bark of the fox will come from across the pond lately made deeper by the beaver. And if perchance snow falls, mouse track and rabbit track will write continued stories for him in every direction, while the underways of mouse and mole and shrew cross in unsuspected numbers.

One comes to regard the birds with affection, there seem to be so few in the deep wood, though the clearings know the old favorites. A white-throated sparrow in some lonely lowland place, a chickadee on some snowy peak, becomes for the moment a comrade. Even the ill-bred jay is welcome about camp. There are over a hundred species that a man can count during the year, yet only a few of these stay for the long winter, and can be called Adirondack birds.

One does not have to be a naturalist to become

Photo by Warwick S. Carpenter

AUSABLE CHASM

acquainted with the wild creatures of the Great North Woods. Just to be a nature-lover is enough. It gives a thrill to twilight, the knowledge that they are there. Not to see them, except the rare shadow of some sleek body, only to hear occasionally some disembodied call in the dark, and yet to know that the ravines and lake shores are haunted by thousands of beautiful animals, draws the fringe of fairyland very close. And some day—who knows?—out of the still great and mysterious reservoir of the north may come back the other beasts, the panther and the wolf.

CHAPTER IX

THE GOSPEL ACCORDING TO PAUL SMITH

THE crisp and stable autumn weather cast a glamour over our travels. Even Luggins, whose strong personality was always hinting at an untimely repose, accepted his pack with dignity if without ardor. Our mode of life had toned our muscles until a decent day's work was a positive gratification to the senses. Two days' cross-country brought us from Childwold to Paul Smith's.

Some men take their vacations in the country and in the deep woods because of their delight in the beauty and stillness and largeness of open distances, while others travel and cling to cities because they are too lonely without the press of personality about them. Dr. Johnson was as emphatically of this type as Thoreau or Muir were of the other. Consequently we find the pages of one sprinkled with flowers and mountains with barely a hint of man unless it be of his imperfections, while the other's book is crowded with the street and there is never a glimpse of the sky.

This relation between physical beauty and human life was a topic that Lynn and I never got quite tired of discussing before our evening fire. We always ended by agreeing that scenery should have only honorable mention if personality was competing. We agreed that we would rather see John Muir than all Alaska, much rather Cleopatra than the Nile.

Because of this tendency on our part and because we had already fed upon about as much scenery as we could hold, the northwest sector of the Park remains for me a beautiful, but unasserting, background against which stand out several amazing personalities.

The background, however, remains fixed firmly in the memory of those days. The entire country is a maze of lakes and hills clustered about the Saranacs and the St. Regis. The hills only rarely earn promotion to mountainhood, but here and there majors are dotted about, with Ampersand a sort of brigadier-general to the south.

While there is considerable cleared land for farms in the neighborhood of the railroads and villages, and while there is even a trolley, the country has only partly lost its claim to wilderness. Wealthy owners have maintained the wooded beauty of the shores that they own. Preserves show great continuities of forest. The Commission is buying in land at every opportunity and reforesting it. Only a little way back from the corner stores you can get your spiked buck in the autumn. The advantages of not despoiling the wilderness further are so clearly seen that the tendency to keep and even extend it can be said to be under way. The period of exploitation is being succeeded by the age of conservation, and right glad were we to find it out.

When Paul Smith died in 1912 he left an estate of 25,000 acres, which included ten lakes, a hotel, a casino, and outlying cottages and camps, besides much money in the bank. When he started life on the St. Regis in 1859 he had a good physique a parent or so to help, and nothing else. Paul Smith, therefore, did his best to preserve the American tradition of the self-made millionaire. There were several reasons why he did not reach the White House and several more why he cannot even be called great. But his reputation will be long in fading away.

Paul Smith's father was a New England lumberman, and his son was twenty-seven years old before he decided that life on the other side of Champlain was not going to yield him the biggest returns. He had a passion for the outdoor life that was over and beyond his professional ardor. On a hunting trip into the Adirondack country his nature was so stirred by the amount of game and timber in the unbroken woodland that he decided to move over. This was accomplished a decade before Gettysburg, doubtless without much embarrassment of paraphernalia. At no time in his life was Paul hindered in his movements by pianos, libraries, and works of art. He settled on Loon Lake.

Soon he discovered the greater beauties of the St. Regis country and settled finally there in 1859. In those days the North Woods would have satisfied a Muir for wildness and a Burroughs for beauty. Toll of the great trees had not been taken by lumbermen or fires. Sportsmen or summer tourists had not made inroads upon the wild life. Wolves were still howling, and the railroad was sixty miles from the cottage that Paul Smith built for his wife. Life there, particularly in winter, was an adventure not continuously easy. But the hazards and difficulties merely emphasized the differences from town life. Anybody who could keep up a contempt for loneliness could be fairly happy there with his dog and gun and wife.

Paul Smith corresponded roughly to the popular conception of a British innkeeper, old style. He was large of build, ate largely, drank, but not too copiously, joked, but not too grossly. His humor apparently spared neither servant nor guest, yet it could not have offended, for from the first his boarding-house grew steadily. Like an English squire he would carve the roast and then go out (as no Englishman below a lord could ever do) and shoot the next meal from his porch. Dr. Trudeau gives an intimate picture in "An Autobiography," saying:

> I can see him in the center of the little dining-room, after having put out his hounds in the morning hunt, beaming with good nature and standing in his shirt-sleeves, with four or five dog chains still slung over his shoulders, carving the venison or roast for his guests and joking with everybody around him.

It is not difficult to see why he should have attracted a clientele. He was an expert guide; his holdings ran with game; his wife saw to it that there was enough of the best to eat. It is difficult to see, however, why a man like that, easygoing, good-natured, not too hospitable to the uncompanionable virtues, should escape from being "done." Many a rich man formed the habit of going into Paul Smith's for a little hunting. But nobody got the better of him in transactions. He took options on desirable lands before the capitalists were quite sure that they were desirable. He bought the water powers on the Saranac River before it was rated anything more than a stream to fish in. He gathered the leading guides about him, and his abilities over the learned and unlearned alike made him a trifle impatient with the world of books, arts, and universities. I cannot believe, however, that it was so much smartness on the part of this indolent and joke-loving woodsman that made him, bit by bit, the most influential landholder in Franklin County. I believe that it was his faith in his own desires that earned him the reputation for farsightedness. Obedience to this faith was the gospel according to Paul Smith.

There is an inertia of content that sometimes moves one further along the road to success than will the most agile endeavors. Paul Smith sat still upon the acres that he had chosen for his heart's desire; his wife cooked appetizing meals, and the wealth of cities came to him and made him rich. He did n't sit with his eyes closed. But he sat, surrounded by the woods that he knew could not fail him, sure that some day his nature's craving for that sort of thing would be vindicated, world-style, by a bank account. His faith pulled through.

That is what I mean by the gospel of Paul Smith. It may not be so noble as the inspired frenzies of his neighbor, John Brown, or the courageous efforts of his boarder, Edward Livingston Trudeau. But there was a moment when the young fellow had to decide whether or not to cast his lot in with the wilderness he loved. There were many moments, doubtless, when these race instincts seemed opposed to common-sense. But he stood firm. And it takes a great man to stand by his instincts. Nearly everybody does take thought for the morrow.

It is a matter for regret that Apollos Smith did

not keep a diary. The span of his life in the woods bridged their entire modern growth. His encounters as a guide with wolves and catamounts, his experiences with Trudeau and Harriman, his love of the wild coupled with his acquisitiveness, would have shot off suggestions of the greatest interest. If he had had the introspection of a Thoreau, the long winter nights in his greater seclusion might have furnished forth a greater Walden. As a matter of fact he spent them playing cards. If he had had the curiosity of an Agassiz, what might his rambles not have brought forth? But Paul Smith, as God created him, as the woods nurtured him, and as the years brought him to a wise old age, was sufficiently distinguished. He would have been valuable enough in the almighty scheme of things if the only flowering of his life had been his kindness to Dr. Trudeau.

Paul Smith's was the one place in the world where the "Beloved Physician" could be sure of recovering from the disease that nearly laid him in the grave each winter. Scarcely a chapter of his autobiography fails to mention the great pines, the beautiful lake to which the sufferer would be carried on a mattress by strong guides, and from which in a few weeks he could return, strengthened, to his life work of strengthening others. In many a chapter there is tribute to the housewifely influence of Paul's wife, as well as to the sympathy

Photo by Warwick S. Carpenter

THE PEAK OF MCINTYRE FROM TAHAWUS' TOP

and kindness that they and their sons extended to the Trudeaus in trouble.

Trouble besieged the Trudeaus. The fight that the doctor put up against his illness for forty years would have been a sufficient example to the world of courage, a sufficient use for his life. But when one considers that without wealth or strength or scientific backing this man established the first line of defenses throughout our country in the war against tuberculosis, any words of appreciation or praise become puny beside the statement of the fact. Trudeau was born in New York City in 1848, and it is significant that his father was so devoted to wilderness life that his devotion to it wrecked his professional career. On one occasion he went off on a long trip with Audubon and is often mentioned in his work. Trudeau inherited the passion for the outdoors and when he discovered, at the age of twenty-four, that he had tuberculosis, he determined to take to the woods where he could end his days hunting.

The days, however, did not end. He regained enough strength to come back to his wife and child, and practised for the winter, only to have another collapse. Paul Smith's pulled him through once more, but his city life again nearly killed him, and after a try at Minnesota he moved his wife and children into Paul Smith's for the winter.

It seemed the most foolhardy of moves. Doctors were unanimous in declaring cold climates fatal to the tubercular. Paul Smith's, moreover, was sixty miles from the nearest doctor. But the spell of the place was so strong on the invalid, his faith in the efficiency of that which he loved was so strong, that he profited by the winter. Another chapter in the gospel according to Paul Smith! Instinct had brought to the first man wealth, to the second health, to both happiness.

The next winter, because Paul Smith and his wife had bought a hotel in Plattsburg, Dr. Trudeau and his wife took a guide's cottage at Saranac Lake. It was a momentous step. Out of it grew the great sanitarium after which hundreds have been modeled, bringing relief to over a hundred thousand patients yearly.

The story of the sanitarium, the struggles against prejudice, the lack of money and strength, the fire, and the death of a son and daughter are told with a moving simplicity in the autobiography. It is a heroic tale modestly put forth. There is a dual impression left on the reader. One reads with the apprehension of suffering on every page. But also on every page is the glow of unselfishness on the part of others. The book is illuminated by the doctor's long sacrifice, by the wealth of love manifested in many relations.

His chapter about his most famous patient

makes good reading, Stevenson having spent the winter of 1887-8 in the Baker Cottage. Trudeau says "the impression of his striking personality, his keen insight into life, his wondrous idealism, his nimble intellect, his inimitable vocabulary in conversation, has grown on me more and more as the years roll by." Trudeau states how he and Stevenson continually had heated discussions because their points of view were so widely at variance. Other observers have told how these illustrious gentlemen parted almost at the point of blows, only to patch it up next day. Each recognized the other's genius intellectually if not sympathetically. Each was not quite fair to the other.

I have discovered no reference to Trudeau in the published correspondence of R. L. S., but his observations concerning Saranac are of interest to remember when you are there.

> The place of our abode is Saranac Lake in the Adirondacks; it is a mighty good place too. . . . It seems a first rate place; we have a house in the eye of many winds, with a view of a piece of running water—Highland, all but the dear hue of peat—and of many hills—Highland also, but for the lack of heather.
>
> . . . .
>
> I remain here in the cold which has been exceeding sharp, and the hill air which is inimitably fine.
>
> . . . .
>
> We are in a kind of wilderness of hills and firwoods and boulders and snow and wooden houses. . . . The climate is gray and harsh but hungry and somnolent. . . . The country is a

kind of insane mixture of Scotland and a touch of Switzerland and a dash of America and a thought of the British Channel in the skies.

. . . .

You cannot fancy how sad a climate it is. When the thermometer stays all day below 10 it is really cold; and when the wind blows, O commend me to the result. Pleasure in life is all delete. There is no red spot left, fires do not radiate, you burn your hands all the time on what seems to be cold stones. . . . We like a room at 48; 60 we find oppressive. Yet the natives keep their holes at 90 or even 100.

A bleak, blackguard, beggarly climate of which I can say no good except that it suits me and some others of the same persuasion whom (by all rights) it ought to kill. It is a form of Arctic St. Andrews, I should imagine, and the miseries of forty degrees below zero with a high wind have to be felt to be appreciated.

These are the references to Saranac with a few others of the same purport; there is no news of Trudeau, no sarcasms at the expense of the many visitors, welcome or unwelcome, no very loving descriptions of the beautiful barbarities about him. There is many an excuse. Stevenson was not really ill at Saranac, according to Trudeau, but half an invalid. He was there only in winter. His memories of the south of France were too vivid to allow an immediate transfer of enthusiasm to "the insane mixture" of the old countries. From all these counts we know why the great romancer has given us but thumb-nail sketches of this most romantic country.

For there is one bit of history, at least, that

transcends American fairy tale in its weavings of court and wilderness, royalty and Indian brave. A year before the French Revolution burst upon an astonished nobility there was formed in Paris *La Compagnie de New York,* an organization intended to forward some settlements already begun in Castorland,—as they called the Beaver-hunting Country,—a tract covering 610,000 acres from Lake Ontario eastward through Lewis and Jefferson counties into the heart of the wilderness.

The Revolution of '93 gave impetus to the attempt, for the clergy and nobility of the old régime could put their only hope for safety in the very wildness of the banks of the Black River. A prospectus was got up, shares sold (fifty-acre lots for $150 each), and a commission came to America. A settlement was effected at Lyons Falls and another at the present Beavertown, then called Castorville.

The commission finally despaired of success in the intractable wilderness, sold out to the Comte de Chaumont, who, employing Fenimore Cooper's father for an agent, built a chateau at Le Rayville, ten miles east of Watertown's present site, and there entertained the exiled nobility of France. One can only imagine the contrasting emotions of the courtiers' gold lace and the gaunt pines; of the gay repartee and the call of the great barred owl mingling to make a fugitive princedom in the wild.

Chaumont went back to France on a visit, and in the year of Waterloo, Joseph Bonaparte, who was looking for a bed of guaranteed repose, met him, dined him, and in the middle of the meal said:

"I remember well you spoke to me of your great possessions in the United States. If you have them still, I should like very much to have some in exchange for a part of that silver I have there in those wagons and which may be pillaged at any moment. Take four or five hundred thousand francs and give me the equivalent in land."

The count gave him 118,000 acres about the present Diana, which name the King bestowed. As you can easily appreciate after seeing the country, rolling remorselessly in one little range after another, it was a land interesting to a hunter, but disappointing to one trying to plot out an estate. A friend wrote of the ex-monarch. "He regrets, notwithstanding that thus far he has been unable to find among the 26,000 acres of land, a plateau of 200 acres to build his house upon, but he intends keeping up his researches this summer."

Bonaparte came over to Jersey and lived in the neighborhood of Bordentown. He built a hunting lodge on the shore of his lovely lake on the Adirondack plateau. To-day it is on the western edge of the forest, but its clean rocky shores and charming islands still hint of the appeal it must have made to the royal fugitive. He put up a summer house where Alpina is now, and at Natural Bridge on the Indian River he built another summer house with bullet-proof rooms which you can still see.

At one despairing time the great Napoleon cast longing glances in the direction of his brother's forest freedom. Chaumont at his chateau near the Black River even discussed the project with Joseph and the son of Maréchal Murat of having a concentration of Bonapartes on that river with the end of establishing vast interests to out-manufacture England. What the State of New York (which passed a special act enabling the royal alien to hold real estate) would have said when it saw the indefatigable ex-emperor involving it in new disputes with Britain need not be imagined because the scheme was dismissed. St. Helena soon shattered the imperial will that might have changed American destinies from its new capital in the wilderness.

Less dazzling, but more substantial, personalities have broiled their bacon by these northern ponds. A group of Cambridge friends spent one summer at Follensby Pond which is below Ampersand Mountain, and another on Ampersand

Pond. They bought 22,500 acres for $600 and intended to philosophize there for their remaining summers, but the Civil War cut the philosophizing short. And now listen to the roll-call: Louis Agassiz and Wyman, his fellow-scientist, Gray, and Dr. Howe, Oliver Wendell Holmes's brother John, Judge Hoar, Stillman, who tells us about it all, and Lowell, and Emerson. Longfellow wouldn't go because Emerson did. I am sorry for Henry W.

Never since Omar outlined his program for a good rest in the wilderness with a little able conversation on the side has the thing been pulled off so satisfactorily. If you can, imagine what they talked about while they were doing up the dishes. Cabbages and kings, no doubt, and also evolution and trout flies and the meaning of meaning. I suppose the paucity of literature turned out by this sparkling crowd of writers must be blamed on the dishes. However, it isn't every holiday diary that rests immortal as does Emerson's "Adirondacs."

Unfortunately the cabin of the Philosophers' Club has disappeared, while Bonaparte's bullet-proof shanty, Paul Smith's hotel, Trudeau's sanitarium, remain. But the beliefs strengthened by those visits to the wildwood: Agassiz's faith in the conception of creation by design, Emerson's passionate search for the nature-powers behind

Photo by Warwick S. Carpenter

MOUNT COLVIN AND SAWTEETH FROM THE AUSABLE CLUB

the veil—these will outlast hotels or the need for sanitaria.

. . . .

The interesting but arduous overland trip from Childwold to Paul Smith's had left Luggins very desirous of resigning from the party. So we housed him comfortably and expensively and took unto ourselves a canoe to see if we could recapture some of the pleasures of our Raquette trip. The scene had changed. The woods were not only a riot of color; they were a rebellion in rainbow, a revolution in French shades. I did not know that so many variations of scarlet, mauve, vermilion, amber, purple, and apoplexy existed. I doubt if an artist could have spent two hours with us on that excursion and survived. The days, too, made for energetic paddling. They were short, but brisk.

From Paul Smith's there are a score of ponds to visit and at least two continuous trips: the "Round Trip" by half a dozen little carries to Upper Saranac and back by some other carries; and the trip to Loon Lake. This latter we took. From Osgood Pond we paddled down a stream, which hadn't any right to the name, and into Lucretia Lake.

Lucretia's endearing young charms are probably a lure for mud-turtles, but the swamp grass and marshy shores scarcely hurry one into sublimity. We passed an inhabitant dredging for fish, pickerel I suppose, although it was late for the best successes. He was drab and bedraggled and a comic contrast to the flaming landscape. But he had a restless humor underscored with drawl.

"Wa'al no," he replied, "I ain't had what you might call luck. This pond 'ere used ter be called Jones Pond and yu' could get a nice bit of fish. But some of them city folks thought Jones was n't a swell enough name. So now they calls it Lucretia Lake, and the fish is got too fussy to take a holt."

A short carry brought us to Rainbow Lake. Nobody who could see it on an October morning would change its name. The shores danced with color, and from an airplane the arc of the lake would make a charming silver bow. The three-mile paddle decided us upon lunch, and after that a succession of tedious and not too beautiful ponds landed us on Loon. The trip is not to be recommended for any particular satisfaction other than the one we had of having made the whole hundred and few miles from Blue Mountain, the longest straightaway in the Park.

Ever since our first days in the Park I had been nursing a secret ambition to buy a little land, to plant one foot in Paradise. I had looked upon the landscape with two eyes, one for its beauty and one for its purchasability. Ruggedly had I refrained from more than inquiry until I had seen the whole stock of goods; just as ruggedly had I examined much territory with care, determined that no supreme bargain should escape me. Therefore when we had arrived at Loon Lake, and the map revealed alluring expanses of wilderness still to the northward, I must needs see it. The water route had run out; Luggins was enjoying an earned vacation. So for the first time in eleven weeks we subjected ourselves to the mortification of a railroad ticket. It read to Lyon Mountain.

The Chateaugay Lake country viewed from the railroad seems well covered with second-growth forest. The mountains are chiefly low rolling ridges. The two lakes join and afford a paddle of eleven miles. Their shores are beautifully wooded, and the views to the southward are sharply cut. It was satisfying to us to see this country, and we could believe the men we asked who asserted that the hunting and fishing to the west were as good as anywhere within the Park. But we did not buy. Neither did we (at that time) go on to Chazy Lake, to the east of which the country rapidly flattens out to the plains around Plattsburg. Instead, the overwhelming homesickness for the woods that strikes hardest at the sight of a starched collar struck. We cut short our inquiries.

Sentiment suggested one more excursion from

Paul Smith's—a drive in a buggy over to Saranac on the exact route that Trudeau had traversed so many hundreds of times in cold and heat, in all the urgencies of illness. Let the doctor speak of the situation of his sanitarium:

> Beyond a jutting projection of the hill was a little level piece of ground, my favorite fox runway, where I had spent many months while hunting with Fitz Hallock, which was always perfectly sheltered from both the south and west winds. Here the mountains, covered with an unbroken forest, rose so abruptly from the river and the sweep of the valley at their base was so extended and picturesque that the view had always made a deep impression upon me. Many a beautiful afternoon, for the first four winters after I came to Saranac Lake, I had sat for hours alone while hunting, facing the ever-changing phases of light and shade on the imposing mountain panorama at my feet and dreamed the dreams of youth; dreamed of life and death and God, and yearned for a closer contact with the Great Spirit who planned it all, and for light on the hidden meaning of our troublous existence. The grandeur and peace of it had ever brought refreshment to my perplexed spirit.

Saranac Lake Village is a city, now, and we were glad to leave it with our new flannel shirts in which we were intending to sport about on sterner heights. So regretting that we could not climb Ampersand or invest in a deer hunt in the northwest forest or allow Luggins further to indulge his passion for overeating at our expense, we left the great waterways of the Adirondack Park and set out for what might befall us in the mountains.

CHAPTER X

LAKE PLACID AND AN EXPERIMENT IN INTELLIGENCE

OCTOBER had had but a short start of us, and the sun not any before we were pointed toward Placid. October's start was a bold one. The clear night had left a film of ice on the smaller ponds; tiny streams breathed mistily in the woods, and along the road the frost lay audaciously in wait for the sunbeams. Clear coffee and fine air put adventure in our blood, and our pace smartened as we went. Only Luggins seemed reluctant. Has nobody tried coffee with horses in the effort to eradicate a certain inertness?

We were ready for adventure, but adventure never retired more coquettishly from road-curve to road-curve. We ceased to gaze wistfully ahead. No fox crossed in front of us; the birds had gone to Dixie. The whole landscape was waiting for something that did not transpire. Apertures in the woodway gave views of forget-me-not and forest green. The scents of sheltered sun patches drifted by us. But never a sound except of Luggins striking an occasional stone in the sandy road! So Lynn and I fell into an appropriate silence. It was no time, we instinctively felt, for incompetent comment on the universe.

Our map plainly pointed to the route through Gabriels, Harriettstown, Saranac Lake, and Ray Brook as the most plausible, even though it stood Luggins a good twenty-five miles. But to round Whiteface by Franklin Falls and up through the Wilmington Notch had the advantage of scenery and an extra day in flannel shirts. That decided us.

To make a bare breast of it, a haze of distrust fell on us when we thought of surrendering to the club. To be sure, the Lake Placid Club had long been a name to us. Hearsay and inquiry had developed its reputation till we had decided upon the ordeal of staying there a week. The necessary cards were in my treasure bag. But for all that, in our separate souls we hated to diminish our summer freedom by three nights in a bed. It was not that we had been too proud to wash; we had despised to advertise in starch. All summer we had collaborated with comfort and wood-sense. We supposed that in a club, comfort must disappear before convention. Even for the purpose of investigation, which was a purpose become dear to both of us, we loathed the idea of being hustled into appearances for a club's sake. To forsake pine-needles for polished floors, an open fire for a radiator, camp costume for evening-dress—these anticipations threw us into such a ditch of despondency that we seized upon the detour with vehemence. Our lightened hearts took us far down the Saranac.

Of all the memories of that day, the green ranges ahead, the high ridges on the right, dipping to let Whiteface look over, the falls, the vast landscapes of brilliant foliage, the spell of the winding road, of all these entrancements there is one that struck deeper than all—the slim, elusive stream of the river, curving in amber shadows, lying at the feet of pointed firs, rippling in a break of light. Noon in such a place is more beautiful than moonlight in many another.

We kept on till mountain shadows and airs, which shivered through disrobing birches, warned us of the piles of fire-wood needful for a long night.

In the morning my thermometer registered twelve. Such tricks will clear air play at the altitude of two thousand feet. But we were not cold. If the breeze bit, his wound healed quickly. Luggins courted the ashes, but we each chopped a log in two and preached him a sermon upon the text. He listened in repose.

More exhilarating than winning bets was it to wash one's face in the brooklet. The glow of the new sun slanted through forests of gold-leaf, for we had tented in a grove of beech. A breath was life, full and undisguised. And later, when smells of breakfast filled the wood, I doubt whether Adam's personal recollections of the new world could have been happier or more vivid.

Up from the Saranac down to the Ausable, then the flank of Marble Mountain, a turn to the right, and we were confronted by the Notch. The Wilmington Notch is the result of the west branch of the Ausable River having its own way, cheeseknife fashion. It has also had its own time, for these are very hard mountains to cut through. It is still going at the job with energy. Above the notch it chatters, becomes more argumentative, and soon downright passionate, till in a great outburst it thunders down and over at High Falls. And all the while it is gnawing at the Notch. Only a long way below the flume does it flow out into carved meadows, forgetful of precipices, black rocks, and the tangle of white waters.

But more interesting than the falls and the gorge was the cold flow of air from the floor of the higher valley before us, and the sight of icicles that would so soon flower into the great winter stalactites. Winter had already established his depot. We were glad to come up into the smiling sun.

As the mountain flanks parted, we came upon

The Ausable River

AN EXPERIMENT IN INTELLIGENCE 237

new and fairer views than any we had seen, splendid prospects of valley floor, curving river, and distant ranges. Our hearts softened toward the club that could revel in such possessions.

In barest terms the Placid valley is a low-undulating river-bottom, checkered with farms and woodland, and walled in on three sides by mountains, on the fourth by a brace of lakes. But the barest terms or the most minute descriptions would fail to convey the circle of landscape from the eye to the ear. So I can best report on an inspiration that fell upon us that autumn afternoon.

We had come on our road to the man-proof fence that surrounds the Club precincts. A little runt of a mountain, which we afterwards found was called Cobble, rose invitingly at our backs. The sun slept on its bare top, which did not look more than ten minutes above us. We determined to spy out the land, tied Luggins to the gate, and in eight minutes by the watch were sitting on the top.

It was the most astounding eight minutes' worth of climb that I have ever done. And many times since have I been up Cobble, once with thunder stalking down the valley, often with the spruces showing black against deep snow, and always there has been some measure of surprise at such a view from such a tiny hill. That first largess of unexpected beauty laid hold of our hearts. We lay there gulping down the distractions of its variety.

Below us, calf-size, stood Luggins, patient with his pack, on the road that wound from the Notch which partly showed to the northeast. The Notch was steeped in shadow; but the sheer range of the Sentinel Mountains, still lighted by the level sun, streamed southward from it, making a barrier all along the east of the valley, an abrupt limit to its beautiful floor. On the south the greater mountains, Elephant, Saddleback, Basin, Haystack, Tahawus, Algonquin, and colder Iroquois stood remote, but clearly high. On the west nearer mountains continued the valley's wall to the break wherein the Saranacs lie. With the proper sun their glimmer can be caught. Again to the northwest McKenzie, Moose, and St. Armand rose protectingly. In the north Whiteface, always noble, dominated. At his foot lay Lake Placid, balsam-girt, islanded.

This then is the skeleton of the view from Cobble. But the form and flesh of the encircling mountains, the flow and color of the valley plain, these no drivel of words can in the least reveal.

Reluctantly, we rose from the rocks. And shadowly we came down through the evergreen to Luggins, and raggedly did we file through the Club grounds, a maze of pine and balsam, and between

AN EXPERIMENT IN INTELLIGENCE

snug cottages to Forest Hall. We presented our cards of introduction from a friend. At once were we received as guests within a family.

It was evident that we had reached the unusual in clubs. Indeed, for a place where your preconception varies more widely from the reality, I know not where to look. Lynn confided to me that his first satisfaction was the broad hearth. We, in our flannel shirts and lumbermen's socks, were not stared at; that was mine. A gentleman-clerk inquired after our trip, a gentleman-bell-boy took our knapsacks. With the courtesy of an acceptance he refused a tip. From this marvel began my study of the Club. I am still studying it.

By bedtime that night Lynn and I had reached an acute stage of curiosity as to the genesis of an institution that performed so many unusual services for its members with such an engaging efficiency. The destiny of any enterprise depends on its objective, its dream, and that upon its dreamer. We longed to meet the person or group of persons who had dreamed this bold and embracing enterprise into being.

Many a time since that autumn evening has the Club been my home. Each time I have seen its significance enlarged, another of its possibilities brought to light. And now despite the dangers of cold type,—false emphasis, chiefly,—the charm and value of the Club are riding me into print.

THE ADIRONDACKS

If I needed excuse it would be that no summary of the features of the Adirondack Park would be complete without mention of this, its most original association. And if I am charged with enthusiasm I can but say that no honest mention could ever be perfunctory.

The Lake Placid Club was sired by a sneeze. For, though at the age of forty-five Melvil Dewey had planted and seen sprout the seeds of more original and useful enterprises than most Americans achieve at ninety, he couldn't resist the spasms of hay-fever. He had started, in 1876, the American Library Association, the American Library Bureau, the Library Journal, the American Metric Bureau, and the Spelling Reform Association. I have forgotten what his business was. Also he had married a woman who had a penchant for starting things too. She started the American Home Economics Association. But she had rose-cold and she couldn't stop that. Thus between sneezes and snuffles this efficient couple lost about four months a year. A birth of a son who might have both diseases determined them. They decided to start something in the Adirondacks.

The Adirondacks has always been a good place for dreams. Old Mountain Phelps had one. He sat on a log and indulged it. If Charles Dudley Warner had not nosed it out, the world would have been little the wiser. Paul Smith had one.

AN EXPERIMENT IN INTELLIGENCE

Even with his parents upon his back, he never lost sight of it. He died rich and respected. Dr. Trudeau had one, a tremendous one. He helped the ailing and the unaided to health, himself neither rich nor in health. And Melvil Dewey has one: perhaps it is the biggest of all.

Now the way of the dreamer is hard. For it is extremely easy to enfog your whole system with the beauty of your dream, vaguely hoping that it may sometime crystallize about your person. That is the way of the amateur dreamer. But the professional's way is different. He begins with some nucleus of fact, some practical act at hand, and wraps his dream about that, irresistibly, no matter how small the progress, how tedious the process. By this time the Deweys were no longer amateurs at dreams.

Their nuclear idea was to set up a sort of university club in the wilderness where men from the colleges might assemble in summer, sneezelessly, and yet undivorced from the agreeable. It was planned for men whose incomes were not too great a match for their intelligences. The meals cost a dollar a day. During the first summer thirty ate them.

They ate them in the Adirondacks only after the entire continent that flies the Stars and Stripes had been searched for a better spot. Maine, Florida, Alaska, California, Wisconsin, Vermont,

Michigan, New Hampshire, North Carolina—all had been discarded for some place in the Adirondacks, and after three more years of inquiry that place had not been located. But Melvil Dewey, once snatched from earth by an idea, was past recapture. He continued hunting.

At last he consulted Paul (who was Apollos) Smith, the sage and father of the Adirondacks, sitting, aged and bent at the top of his stairway. At first the old guide would not admit that there existed finer sites than his St. Regis lakes and lands. But being pressed, he said finally,

"Well, Dewey, everybody knows there ain't a finer place in the hull woods than Placid, but after that you 've got to come here."

Upon those words, as in novels, the sneezer and wife took guide and canoe, went through the seven carries, climbed into their buckboard, drove twenty-odd miles through arching wood, and when they stood on that little hill by Mirror Lake and looked over the rolling valley to its enclosing ranges, they knew that their New World had been discovered. At that time there were few houses at Lake Placid. But in them dwelt the crafty. They demanded a thousand dollars an acre for the best of their land.

In those days, 1890, any amount of land could have been bought for $500, $200, $50, $10 an acre, and the Deweys spent more summers roaming about in the hopes of making a lucky strike, but always they returned to Placid. The crafty ones had raised their views on the value of their soil to $2500 an acre. It speaks well for the texture of the dream that only the best was good enough. Mr. Dewey got a better price at wholesale, and took 250 quarter-acres. At last the dream was housed.

For the next twenty years the solidifying of shadows, the expansion on new planes took place. It was not without compromises, defeats, labor, that complete disaster was staved off. There was much ebb and flow of check-book, much silent sacrifice, much hope.

During the second summer the wilderness university club was visited by eighty guests, while last August there were eleven hundred guests at once, not counting the seven hundred employees, and many others disappointed for lack of room. Numbers, of course, mean little. Eleven hundred guests at Coney Island, for example, would not excite comment other than profane. But eleven hundred at a club that is still very much in the woods, every one of them vouched for by a member or his friend, and no one of whom but is in sympathy with the lines of club development imposed by an energetic and elevating dream—eleven hundred guests of this kind is a triumph-in-sort.

I believe the clue to Mr. Dewey's dream can be found in something that underlay his previous endeavors. His names for his library association, his library bureau, his metric bureau, and all the rest were prefaced by the word American. It cannot have been by chance. He knew that the men and women who live under the flag can never be either satisfied with life or be true Americans unless they live somewhat in accord with the eternal verities, for of such was the beginning of our nation. It was belief in the eternal verities that gave America her reason for being. She feared God; she was brave; she did not disdain to labor; she was frugal; she admired cleanness, honesty, high-thinking.

What began as the Placid Club was, therefore, more than a refuge for hay-fever victims, more than an eating-resort for indigent intellectuals. It gave men breathing time in surroundings of haunting loveliness. It gave them a chance to cleanse themselves, to see things squarely, to come into high thoughts. And almost the only essential for membership was character. No matter how prominent or able or wealthy a man or a woman might be, if she or he had not that passport to good society, which is easier to recognize than to define, that person was asked to seek elsewhere more congenial atmospheres. And every season some such persons, who cannot grow accustomed

Photo by Irving L. Stedman

Tahawus, Algonquin and Iroquois; The Great Range

AN EXPERIMENT IN INTELLIGENCE

to life without a bar, or who mistake the spirit of the Club in other ways, receive such a request. The result is that the atmosphere is kept so unhotel-like that parents who would not leave a child alone in a hotel for a single night have often traveled abroad, leaving their young daughters at the Club for all summer in entire confidence that no unhomelike taint will touch them.

No person can be entertained at the Club without an introduction or invitation from a member. In a private card catalogue under constant revision every guest is rated on his merits and marked by letters. If he belongs to class C, he is a common client, welcome, neither specially advantageous to his fellow clubmen nor at all disadvantageous. If he belongs to class B (better), he has some talent, some distinguishing traits that make him desirable. He is sought for membership. Class A includes those who are admirably suited to further the ideals of the club. They are given every inducement to join. Class D, on the other hand, contains the doubtful or deficient characters, who, if not positively discouraged from joining, are not invited till a further insight into their personalities has been obtained. Class E is made up of unsuitables who, if already in, must be eliminated; if still out, must be excluded for the protection of the rest. It is a pretty game. Thanks to the closeness of the unguessed scrutiny and to the superior level of influence demanded, the easy charm of the place has not had to wane with growing numbers.

An exceptional membership naturally has demanded exceptional service. And before any clerk or bell-boy is engaged, his past is searched for any possible reasons why he should not be attached to the force. Engaged, he knows that however capable he may be, a cigarette, a glass of beer, a deviation into profanity or vulgarity of any sort will send him job-hunting. In this broad country there are men eager for the opportunity to live and work under the best imaginable influences, and the intelligent gladly deprive themselves of cigars and profanity to their profit. They also abjure tips, but as many guests leave or send back parting gifts they lose nothing but the humiliation. Besides being better paid than hotel servants in like capacities, they have better meals, better living-rooms, recreation centers, an occasional motor or launch. A $20,000 staff house is to be built for them. And members continually say that they feel more comfortable knowing that those who minister are well cared for.

The Club's first distinction is character; its second is excellence of equipment. In many departments this nears perfection. Again the essentials have been demanded. Since neither display nor the nonsense of pretension figures in the expense

AN EXPERIMENT IN INTELLIGENCE

account, the club is able to focus its brains and resources on the items of practical advantage. It was supplied with the most invigorating air under heaven; it secured a perfect water supply. Milk was a more difficult matter. Cornell experts found that local sources were all unsound. The club bought a cow and lodged her sanitarily. She has increased five hundredfold, and the amount of cream consumed a month is a matter for comment; no guest is denied any lactic desire. Indeed, the cream and milk, the butter and eggs lay the foundation for a table that is deliberately the best possible within limits. These limits lie well within commonsense and yet well beyond reasonable desire. The range at any meal must take into account the oldish lady who has sat by the fire all afternoon and the men who have been mountaineering on snow-shoes. And from end to end each item must be of the best. I know that there is no hope of saying this without its sounding like an advertisement. Their pastry cooks must be exquisite fellows.

Beds, the management claimed, were of the utmost importance, and all the money should go into springs and mattresses and blankets and none whatever into carvings and guardian angels. The tired ski-er sleeps delightfully. Beds make an excellent hobby for club-makers. And in the infirmary one can lie all day in the last luxuries of healing if tobogganing has disabled or the intoxication of flexible flying been overdone.

Another extravagance is the system of fire protection; $50,000 has been spent to perfect a system that in times of greatest drought or in the wildest blizzard could deluge the first flames with 2500 gallons a minute from its system of hydrants. A night and day patrol is so arranged that a fire could never get a running start; the great fire-pump is kept under constant pressure; Mirror Lake is the supply. Fires do occur. In twenty-three years forty-two have broken out. But the system has kept the total loss under $500. Angry flames, indeed!

And now of the greatest extravagance of all. One day Dr. Albert Shaw of the "Review of Reviews" asked if he might sink a couple of tomato cans in the garden turf to knock a white ball into. In such a manner the game of ten centuries' growth began at Lake Placid. The Club has sunk $200,000 in their turf. Four hundred players have done themselves tan on the courses in one day. And the difficulties begin with the choice of your course; there are four now, three nine-hole courses and one of eighteen holes, of 6300 yards, and two more eighteen holers of 6000 yards are already well under way. The Club dooryard is ten miles long and there is always room. Nowhere in the world in such a setting of great woodlands,

AN EXPERIMENT IN INTELLIGENCE 251

shapely peaks, and passes can men follow the ball over courses more interestingly diversified, more scientifically planned. Even Lynn, whose title for the game is "fugitive idiocy," was soothed into something very like admiration for the technical as well as the natural beauties as explained to us by the creator, Mr. Dunn.

And if this prospect does not hold you spellbound, I, who talk as if the Club were the result of mine own vigil,—I will offer you others. There are forty courts for tennis and other outdoor games, and there is fishing away, and boating at home, and water-sporting, and riding and driving, and camping by still waters, and music and pageants, and four outdoor theaters, and climbs, and the four million acred Park in which to play in company with the most charming people of the land. And it is this last that brings me back from the outlay of dollars to the dream.

How is it, one may reverently inquire, that granted a perfect setting, a perfected apparatus of enjoyment, an atmosphere of commonsense, warmed with culture and kept in motion by great wealth,—how is it that the Lake Placid Club can prevent itself from gradually being enwrapped in a cocoon of complacency, refinement, sport, and soullessness? This conundrum presented itself to us on the second day. A sample bill had been sent around to our room, as is the custom, so that if there are any moments of harsh surprise they may come at the beginning of one's sojourn and not at the end. I believe I had remarked that the place was extraordinary.

"Extraordinary!" said Lynn. "Well, and well it might be. For every day that you and Luggins and I pay our bill we might have a fortnight in the woods. It's easy wallow for the rich, but some pace for the professor. You said that it was founded for the classics who 'd taken the count, did n't you?"

On the following day, I replied:

"It is." I had sought, met, and been conquered by the idealist in the room where he puts his ideals to hard labor. It is a room piled quite high with the paraphernalia of offices and does n't look at all like a den of visions. It is a very practical idealery. And its master is big, well-set, bushy-browed, peering, quick; the garment of his being is that of a purposeful business man. Only when stripped for confidences do you sense the aggressive prophet.

I am glad that I came upon the Club in its success, for the season of strenuous waiting is at an end. At the other end, a quarter of a century back, it would have been too easy to have said with the great majority, "It is a pretty dream, but it will not work."

AN EXPERIMENT IN INTELLIGENCE

The core of the dream was: "by coöperation to secure among congenial people and beautiful natural surroundings all the advantages of an ideal vacation or permanent country home." The congenial people were the worn college professors, "the classics who had taken the count," according to the irreverent Lynn. But I had not seen any of these about. Rosy and exuberant millionaires golfed in droves and hiked long distances. But as a retreat for the professorial élite whose thoughts were longer than their pocket-books the Club was but raggedly utilized. So little was I acquainted with the ways of the practical visionary that I, too, began to think that it was "easy wallow" for the rich and rich alone.

Early in the dreamiest stage the young Club began to lose money. At a critical time one of Mr. Dewey's originations brought him in twenty times what the original Club cost, and he and his wife put that and the rest of their fortune into the dream. Thus do Holy Grailers.

As expansion came more capital was needed, and without abandoning their final object, they called in the millionaire, the intellectual rich man, to make the others' paradise a possibility. The final object was and is a permanent foundation in this most lovely of all regions where the promising youth of the country may lay hold of inspiration and carve it to their uses. The Club is to be, and is, the home of inspiration in practice. Tried intellects will gather on their sabbaticals; assemblies of research will meet; congresses of moment will debate in this most suitable environment. In the cool of summer or in the white fire of winter the country's best will exchange ideas before the open hearth. It would sound too beautiful if the foundation had not been laid and hardened to support the superstructure these many years.

See what has been done: Seventy-five hundred acres owned in the heart of a great and perpetual State park; farms, buildings, camps, sport facilities developed; a large membership culled from two countries, on whom is the impress of the Club's essential ideals; a financial incorporation now beyond the power of individual whim to change; and the creator of all this yet young enough to drive on with the unfinished dream.

Emerson doubtless fed on his own dictum many times without divining how nourishing it would be to others when he said, "If a man can make a better book, preach a better sermon, or make a better mouse-trap than his neighbor, the world will make a beaten track to his door."

This is the motto of the Club. And with its glorious text a sermon is being preached, the purport of which is health, wisdom, and good-fellowship.

Lower Ausable Lake

Photo by Warwick S. Carpenter

October swam over into November while Lynn and I lingered in the lap of bankruptcy at this caravansary. And when we pulled Luggins from his bed of enervating luxury, we three swore that when our chores were done, back we would come in time for winter sports. How my hand itches to be at the naming of them, if only to carry me back to the season when there are no tragic insects, no weeks of mist, and when the winter woods are fair—so fair that I cannot resist the telling, the trying to tell, in its own proper place!

CHAPTER XI

THE GIANTS CLOTHED WITH STONE

OUR fortnight in the Placid valley had made a change for the grimmer in the mountain covering. We had entered it in gold; we were leaving it in gray. Probably six weeks would pass before the great winter snows would fall. Until then the color would die out of everything but the evening skies. It was a waiting season and we would have liked to have waited with it at the Club where a between-seasons idleness encouraged a comradely feeling that the stress of summer could not know. But despite our three months' wanderings, the Adirondacks proper were still before us, still unclimbed. Until we had stood on Marcy we knew we should have that uncompleted feeling for goals unachieved which only Luggins did not indulge.

It was not easy for us to break away. We did want to complete the trip under canvas, but high winter was no longer an adventure; it was a calculation. A sudden drop to anything below zero was within the range of past recordings; we had to go prepared. We had softened, too, with our

THE GIANTS CLOTHED WITH STONE 259

hot tubs and sheeted beds and slave-got breakfasts. Luggins did not regard it as an act of mercy to be filched from his sociable stable to gratify the ambitions of two deranged sight-seers. The hardest thing was to clap a finis to some interesting acquaintanceships at the club. We determined that only drastic methods would get us off at all. So because neither of us fatten on farewells, we made the excuse of a far journey and got away at dawn when most Club members are in their Placid beds.

Two miles from the Club we passed for the last time the little farm, high, bleak, whence sprang the Civil War. There lies John Brown's body a-moldering in the grave. Somehow the valley is bigger for the grave. We stopped for a last look.

Already out of the west low, bellying clouds had begun to sow white flakes before a rising wind. Between the flurries a pale sunshine chased over the valley floor. I have never seen an outlook so bare, so reproachful, so indicative of unconditional servitude. However mad the fragrant, luxurious South may have thought the old abolitionist, if they could have had but one look at his pitiful home, they would have been convinced of his stern sincerity.

John Brown was born in Connecticut in 1800. Fifty-nine years later he was hanged at Harper's Ferry. The story of those years shapes all to the one mad end. It is relentless as is a Greek tragedy. The setting of the story is so bare that it seems as if perpetual November is the right atmosphere of plot and character. There are vines about the house, but doubtless his wife planted those. All souls feel the instinct for beauty. She did not understand her husband's. "He seemed to think there was something romantic in that kind of scenery," she told Mr. Wentworth Higginson. She probably thought it was a very cold romance.

John Brown had so long subjugated his senses, his judgment to his plan for freeing the colored race that he was affected not at all by comforts or discomforts. He was warmed by his idea above the rigors of climate. Fed or not, he had traveled from neighbor to neighbor to give them the final instructions of the raid. For years his living idealism had fissured the stony hearts of his more prosaic neighbors until they were willing to support him and his sons in any venture. While dreaming in the sight of his beautiful mountains, it was possible to believe that impossible salvations would come true. But even for him there must have been moments of doubt. When you see the unpainted barn, when you realize the winter hardships, you can appreciate the high purpose that nursed a great scheme in a country where to support life itself is hard enough. It is the evidence

THE GIANTS CLOTHED WITH STONE 261

of his homely struggle and not the simple carving on the great gray boulder that is so poignant to me. The tragedy is not that he was executed, not even that he should have led his sons to an unuseful death. The tragedy is that after a lifetime of solitary planning he should have died believing that his lifetime's dream had totally miscarried.

The snow flurries increased in violence, and we were glad to leave the barren grave and descend to the river which we crossed despite the incredulity of Luggins. A path led through the woods and out upon the road to Heart Pond. On the road we were hustled manfully in the rear by the wind. The weather was turning colder. When we came out upon the lake, its glare of ice looked as lonely and remote as Baffin Bay.

It is easy to believe that Heart Pond before the forest fire was the supreme gem of the wilderness. The water is said to be incredibly clear. The slopes of the great mountains rise on all sides. Only an unmarred forest is wanting to complete the picture of sheltered loveliness. Even on the blustery day that blew us thither the roar of the gusts on the distant slopes sounded as through a spell, and the sun between whiles shone serenely on us protected by a shoulder to the north called Mount Jo.

The great fire was in 1903, so that the new trees have already half their growth. The Club had bought the land just three years before because it had been pronounced by experts the very finest square mile of woods in all the Forest Preserve's four million acres. There had been an old hunter's inn there which was destroyed, but the fire was extinguished before the trails or the big mountain flanks had been ruined. In a few more years the Club will rebuild the headquarters, constructing a log house in the good taste that makes the hotels of our Western parks an addition to the view instead of necessary eyesores. Now, there are sheds and two or three camps for the small parties which drive out from the Club every day in summer.

The Adirondack Lodge used to be the best starting place for several climbs, all very interesting. And it will be a mountain focus again. More shelters will be built along the trails. Protection by fire-wardens, ownership by clubs, and an increasing public interest in conservation will preserve the wildness and beauty of this block of a hundred square miles in all its grandeur. For charm of situation it has very few equals. For accessibility to the great summits none. From the site of Adirondack Lodge there are trails up the mountains which you climb in from two to seven hours. But ambition rests there. This section can never be used for promiscuous picnicking. So here we have the desideratum of all lovers of the wild: a region of rugged, forested, well-watered beauty, protected by club and State and nature from vandalism forever, so extensive that no one can know it thoroughly, so forbidding that only the accomplished can know parts of it intimately. And for eight months of the year only the most courageous (or foolhardy) will seek to know it at all.

Heart Pond, formerly known as Clear Pond, fulfilled our most exacting tastes, and we set about settling for an indefinite stay. There is something heart-lifting in such a decision. Coziness appeases the cat in us, just as good meals from a stationary stove appease the wolf. I don't know how many other animals there are inside me. But I suspect Lynn and I represent a fairly varied menagerie at times. And Luggins can be such an ass! His judgment, for example, about the amount of fire-wood that ought to be hauled in for a winter's evening is notoriously untrustworthy. If Lynn chops it down and I chop it up, Luggins' share of work obviously is to haul it in to camp. But it has taken a lot of expostulation to convince him of the ignominy of slacking. Some day I hope that they will breed horses with probosces so that, like an elephant moving teak, the camp broncho can assume all responsibility for bringing in the logs.

It was going to be a cold night. Heart Lake is

about 2200 feet above sea level, and the mercury was about that much below freezing. And we had no one to share the cold with. We could keep it all for ourselves. Of the hundred millions residing in the United States 999,998 souls were shoveling coal into their furnaces on that boisterous evening while we were camping out a hundred miles from congested cities, from furnaces, and from coal.

But the ingenuity of young America has not yet been stifled by enervating luxury. We had found a shack with a stove in it. The shack was made of boards and designed for comfort in a Texas summer. The boards kept out the larger masses of air that beat upon the house, but the cracks, which made the wall look very much like a paling fence laid on its side, let in narrow strips of cold. The result gave you the effect of sitting in forty draughts at once. Lynn said that he did n't like his cold striped.

Then he made his suggestion. We had stretched the tent and the floor cloth on the north and west sides of the shack, but had n't clothes enough to dress up the rest of the building. So we had the simple inspiration of putting up the tent inside the shack. By pitching the baker in front of the stove we were soon as comfortable as on a June evening when spring is a little late.

It is a matter for philosophy how great an en-

Photo by Warwick S. Carpenter

SAWTEETH FROM THE UPPER AUSABLE LAKE

THE GIANTS CLOTHED WITH STONE 267

thusiasm a little inspiration kindleth. Sometimes the inspiration is a cup of coffee before you set up camp; sometimes it's a hot stone at your foot at 2 A.M. It almost always is some tiny detail that changes the world for you in a manner that would be touching if it were n't childish. We had been confronted by an Arctic night in a desert waste. We shift a bit of waterproofing. Now we listen to the blasts howling over a magnificent mountain world, happy in their howling. "What fools these mortals be!" is a charitable way of putting it.

We were happy. Luggins was inactive and satisfied. Lynn and I had a great store of wood, a luxury of appetite, and much food. We were about to explore as gratifying a wilderness of peaks, passes, and cascades as our sunlunary sphere can furnish. We dreamed off soon, to the accompaniment of the gale which roared as does the sea at some great cliff. At drowsy intervals during the night I was aware of it surging up to assail the shack with weight.

We woke to find the weather still playing in the same key. The squalls had deposited an inch or two of snow-dust, and there were alternations of sky curtain and deep blues. A big mountain was out of the question, and we wanted to reserve the pass. So we climbed Mount Jo. It rises only a few hundred feet above the pond, but steeply, making a north wall to the lake, and from a bared rock it gives a view of the soaring slopes of McIntyre. Colden, Marcy, and the rest shone out distantly between squalls though their extreme tops were never visible.

That afternoon the wind dropped, followed by the temperature. At the pink of the next morning it registered 4° above zero. But for chopping, flannel shirts open at the neck were an inconvenience. The air affected one like prosperity. Just walking was not good enough. One felt like skipping up McIntyre before breakfast and running over to Marcy on the way home. Plain earth was superfluous support. Bodies were an incumbrance.

We set out, the three of us, for the great adventure of our trip, the crossing of Indian Pass. Advice to us had been divided. Many, while not exactly saying "Fools!" to our faces, had hinted as much when we suggested taking Luggins along. On the other hand a member of the Commission himself had told us that it was possible, though requiring care.

In the sun the light covering of snow was melting, and our progress was not rapid. We ignored the beckoning of the Iroquois Ravine, which leads you up into the recesses of McIntyre. I can recommend the place to any hermit who is particularly greedy for solitude. Farther on, a trail

THE GIANTS CLOTHED WITH STONE

into a pond, Scott's, cuts off to the southwest on the right. The scramble began shortly after that.

We did not get Luggins over. The member of the Commission was right, however. It can be done with a horse without unnecessary danger. But there were three reasons why it seemed unwise to us. The days were almost at their shortest, and we risked having night for the other end. The snow, while only two or three inches deep below, was fully half a foot at the beginning of the real climb and promised to be an actual hindrance above, where a misplaced foot on the part of our carry-all might deprive us of his society in its most useful form. An inch of reason is worth a mile of regret was Lynn's happy paraphrase of Luggins's own opinion about proceeding. So we recavalcaded along the trail to spend another night in the heat-proof shanty.

The next morning was just as cold, just as clear, and we set out before the sun, leaving Luggins smiling at the thought of peace. Before noon we were eating lunch, delicious as well-earned, at the Summit Rock of the Indian Pass. Some day when the Hudson valley is one continuous city and all the rest of the State is suburbs, they will block up the ends of Indian Pass and use it for cold storage. We ate there not to create a record in chills, but because we were famished and the view was fine. But a fire and hot tea and hot beans and hot mush with sugar and heated milk were of little avail against the searching tooth of that type of cold. The enormous cliff and the shadowy chasm and we were all cold and wild together. Whatever the sun may accomplish in midsummer, I can assure any one that its effort in late November is a total loss. If anybody chooses to tell me that the snow does n't melt there all the year round or that ice is found in the caves on the Fourth of July or any of the other tales that accumulate about a superior sort of desolation like the Indian Pass I shall believe him.

The Indians had nerve. The pass on a dark day must be overpowering. The cliff, Wall-Face, goes straight up in the air for exactly a quarter of a mile. Opposite, McIntyre goes a lot higher though not quite as straight up. You walk between them hoping that the rocks which fall now and then, a ton or so at a time, will bound over you. The ravine is choked with them. You can't see the water at the bottom which works its way around the boulders. But you can hear it, they say. We did n't! When we stopped to listen our teeth chattered. But local history tells of nobody being killed by these falling rocks. Even on the other trail where an avalanche fills up a lake every so often, nobody has been killed. Perhaps it is a safety like that of the burro trail down into the Grand Canyon. Nature may disdain the obvious.

THE GIANTS CLOTHED WITH STONE 271

The Indians had nerve, certainly. How did they know that their enemies were n't waiting on the ledges to sprawl landslides on them? How could they be sure that this dark lane was not a lure of the Stonish Giants! To an Indian everything was spiritual or devilish. And I should judge that from appearances the Pass was mainly devilish. It would be in a thunder-storm beyond uncertainty.

It is quite beyond my efforts to describe the impressiveness of this gorge on a serene day in autumn. To have to reproduce a thunder-storm would be a predicament, indeed. The Iroquois called the trail "Path of the Thunderer." They had courage to follow it. The general locality was known to them as "Place Where the Storm Clouds Meet in Battle with the Great Serpent." One can safely imagine the affair from a distance: the black battlements of rock, the strip of livid sky, the Adirondack lightnings, the crash of cliffs and thunder about your head, the falling rain and trees. It would be a noble death.

Lynn and I did not stop to do the dishes, not even the mush pot. For a brief moment the sun had stolen around some corner and had lit up the forest. Before us a million trees merged in a rolling and conglomerate woodland. Behind us was the darkest and narrowest of the Pass.

Of course we had our eyes open for the twin streams whose sources are virtually one, whose endings are as far apart as "No" and "Yes." I wish that we had seen them, for the effect on writers is always lyrical. It makes them unable to say that one stream runs out into the Hudson and that the other gets to the St. Lawrence. It makes them phrase it something like this: "Born in a twin cradle, and flowing side by side for a brief span they soon part forever, one running to mingle its crystal waters with the waves that wash the shores of beautiful Block Island, the other pursuing its boisterous way until it is lost in the salt floods that beat upon the ice-bound coasts of Labrador."

That is a way streams have. I don't know on how many great divides you can find springs flowing into half a dozen oceans at once. In Yellowstone Park there is one; in Glacier Park another; Colorado has two or three. I am glad that the Adirondack Park is not behind them even in this particular.

From Wall-Face the path descends for a couple of hours without any misleading trails until you get to Lake Henderson. We went carefully at first to avoid any pitfalls, but that danger almost disappeared at a lower altitude, and we ran. I believe that running down a mountain is the most common and least defensible crime committed in the woods. Take a beech slope slippery with leaves and full of little trees to brake you as you pass, or take a mountain with six feet of hardened snow, or even take a mountain brook with pitfalls at every leap: there is no wisdom short of an old guide's that will out-argue the fun. And you never get hurt. With a fracture certain at every third step you never twist your ankle. You are keyed to instant response. You soar over sticks; you escape the hole while your foot is pointing into it. And if you misjudge some pile of leaves you skip disaster by omitting a step or two and flying through the air instead. The only danger is moderation. You can get down the tallest mountain in the shortest time by imitating the way the water comes down at Lodore. And only he who hesitates breaks a leg. For sheer exhilaration and variety of risk there is no amusement so heartily to be criticized, so whole-heartedly to be recommended.

Lake Henderson is one of the monuments to an iron merchant; Mt. Henderson is another; the Iron Works is another; his marble shaft is another. It is a sad story, but I shall weep for him on another page, merely saying in passing that it is a rare foundry manager who can have half a landscape named after him.

Adirondack is the site of the dead iron industry which is about to be revived in this section. It is also the headquarters of one of the most important of the Adirondack clubs, the Tahawus, a continuation of the Adirondack Club. This association, assuming charge of some of the most important forested land in the Adirondacks, owning, indeed, most of Marcy and McIntyre and Colden and half a dozen lakes, several sources of the Hudson and one of the Raquette River, has made good its ownership. Everything is preserved as the Commission would have it. Travelers like ourselves are housed for the night when there is room. I should imagine, however, it were better to be prepared to hear that there is no room. I cannot imagine a club member being able to get there and not getting.

In the moonlight we went out on Lake Henderson. The ice was thick enough to harvest. In the dim light McIntyre and Wall-Face and that eerie Path of the Thunderer through which we had come appeared legendary and indistinct. There were no storms now battling with the serpent. The serpent was dormant. But his atmosphere persisted. I insist on the bravery of those Indians.

I find that I have not given the moon her due. Lynn and I spent six moons in the woods and were grateful to each of them. In the city sky a moon is a graceful ornament very much like a coat of arms. You may notice it while stepping from your hotel to your taxi, unless you are blinded by the electric lights. But in the woods it is searchlight,

INDIAN PASS FROM LAKE HENDERSON

Photo by Warwick S. Carpenter

THE GIANTS CLOTHED WITH STONE 277

weather prophet, and society. In the summer it plays enchantment on lovely landscapes. In the winter it livens the inhabitants with its shine. The north star is a surer friend, but for a luxury that fades to come again, let me commend the wilderness moon.

We did not feel that we should take time to visit the Preston Ponds whence the Cold River rises, or go down to Tahawus and out into the Schroon Lake country, or to the Opalescent River which is a name coined out of Heaven, or to the little pond, Tear of the Clouds, the highest source of the Hudson, for Luggins was in the shack alone. Unfortunately Luggins is not a philosopher unless you put him among the Epicureans. His thoughts are not the long, long ones of youth, but the short and distracted ones of a gourmand uncertain about his next meal. Therefore we decided that our duty focussed upon the north shore of Heart Pond. We decided, however, to take the new and easier and longer way back by Avalanche Lake.

The clear weather was holding. It was an easy walk up to the Henderson Monument near Calamity Pond, also dedicated to the memory of the ironmonger. The stone is beautiful. The inscription reads:

"Erected by filial affection to the memory of our dear father, David Henderson, who accidentally lost his life on this spot by the premature discharge of a pistol, 3rd Sept., 1845."

We forgot the calamity in the ascent, and, when that ended, in Lake Colden. We longed to follow its outlet down to the famous "Flume of the Opalescent." The Hanging-Spear Falls must be fine enough, and the contour of the survey map makes for splendid water-rushes. When you take into account the reputed amounts of opalescent feldspar which give the stream in sunlight its sparkle and its name the sight must be worth many dead horses. But Luggins was a friend.

By this time, anyway, we were so impressed by this country that we had been planning a next summer's return, which made it easier to forego the Opalescent. Although the two lakes, Colden and Avalanche, lie in a pass, they get some sun, and we had lunch under different conditions from those of the day before. "A geologist would probably settle here for good," I wrote in my notebook, "because nothing is where it is meant to be, and that makes a geologist happy." Or any kind of a scientist, I might add. Give a scientist something to explain, and he is content. Unfortunately neither Lynn nor I knew anything more about the earth than that it is an oblate spheroid (remembered from youth), so we were unable to appreciate the flinty hypersthenes and trap dikes of Mount Colden. But we could ignorantly admire

THE GIANTS CLOTHED WITH STONE 279

the size of the avalanches that have raced down the sides of that unsettled mountain. One of them filled up the lake in the middle, and they call the other half Avalanche Lake now. The Indians called Colden *Ournawarla,* which means Scalped. We walked down the middle of the lake. I suppose there must be a trail beside it in summer. There did n't appear to be much room for one.

It was still early afternoon when we had finished the five miles from Avalanche to Heart. But we were ready to stop. The round trip is nearly thirty miles, and we had done some other walking too. The light snow had required caution. So there was considerable mutual joy in the ventilated shack. A pony does n't jump up into your lap and lick your face; he does n't even arch his back and purr; but as Lynn put it, "the little old cow can get pretty doggone glad to see you, and it is n't all meal-ticket gladness either."

With the next dawning came signs that the cold and clear wave was about done. The sky was still cloudless, but the north wind was hushed at last; it was a magnificent day for either Marcy or McIntyre, which latter we chose.

On an energetic day McIntyre can be ascended in less than two hours from Heart Pond. We would have done better than two if at the top there had been no snow. But above a certain zone it speedily deepened. Even the trees were slippery with frost. At the steepest it was rather fun hauling yourself up from trunk to trunk in a shower of snow-flour. But it was hard keeping the trail. At the Club we had jotted down instructions and, in winter, contours are easier to follow, but time after time we had to look for blazes when we could discover no signs of cleared way. The falls were silent, owing to the dry autumn and the frost. McIntyre is 5112 feet high, second only to Tahawus's 5344. But such is the pressure of a superlative that ten people struggle up Marcy to every one that tops McIntyre. In my humble opinion Marcy comes about fifth in desirability. From Marcy you have a view of a stupendous jumble. It is like being on top of the biggest bubble in a boiling cauldron. While from Whiteface, from the Giant, and in most directions from McIntyre you have the world laid before you, an out-soaring panorama. From McIntyre on a day such as ours they tell me you can count one hundred and thirty-five lakes.

We had no desire to count. The scene was lovely beyond enumeration. People vary as much at a mile up as they do at sea-level. Some like to sit in a stupor of beatification, some like to get out the map to verify God's handiwork. It will be the same way in Heaven: the sheep will be dazzled by the Throne, while the goats are counting the candlesticks to see if they are seven. I

THE GIANTS CLOTHED WITH STONE

am glad, personally, for the variety. And particularly if you are one of the easily beatified kind, it is a matter of convenience to include a map-worshiper in the party.

There were certain features that began to intrude upon our receptivities after the first ten minutes of vague delight. Tahawus, of course, butted one in the eye, and Colden and the spot of water into which it shakes stones from time to time. Far off to the southwest we saw a strip of silver we guessed was Long Lake. To the north Whiteface had a hoary crown and we could see part of Saranac. Seward rose in dignity to the west, but the thing that caught our eyes was the Wall-Face precipice, not nearly so imposing, however, as from underneath. Indian Lake and a country of rolled green that lifted into edges of blue ran to the southward, and above the line of blue a line of summery looking clouds lay waiting. Overhead filmy mare's-tails drew curved designs across the blue. They promised insurrection on the morrow, but the present was divinely fair. We sat warm as in summer on the summit rock. The thin snow covering radiated back the sun and tanned us like an August sea-shore. Yet while we were making lunch the haze grew thicker on the distant mountains. Finally they withdrew. That night we heard rain falling on our shack.

The first thought instigated by the more enchanting places in the Park was to settle in each one for life. Since that proved inconvenient offhand, the next was to promise ourselves an immediate return for that purpose. Consequently there are at least half a dozen localities where we are engaged to spend the rest of our days. Heart Pond is one of these. Not right in that shack, understand, but at a little distance where angels come, but do not trouble the water in order not to frighten the trout.

But we left the next day. Mists fell far down the slopes of McIntyre and even rested on Mount Jo. Instead of following the road back to North Elba, we noticed a trail that would bring us to the neighborhood of the Cascade Lakes. I have passed over the ground that we omitted since. In a winter blast the open plain is such an exact reproduction of a Siberian tundra that experts would be confused. There is one point of historical interest: the expanse of land left by a Mr. Gerrit Smith for the benefit of negroes. There were one hundred thousand acres of it. Mr. Smith presumably had never had a tropical ancestry or he would not have expected the colored race to dwell on that plateau. Equatorial blood is much too thin for our north intemperate zone at its best. But life on that piping plain in a nor'wester would make an Eskimo double his ra-

THE GIANTS CLOTHED WITH STONE 283

tion of tallow candles. I have seen the snow drive across it in the middle of May, the stage horses frosting at the mouth and the driver praying to St. Nick. Only in July on its waterless expanse does the mercury take a consistent interest in the upper register. And then the sandy levels make a very fair imitation of the Little Sahara. A good many families took advantage of Mr. Smith's offer. But there was a mix-up in the deed; bad law froze out a good many, the weather more, until to-day on the entire grant only one colored family survives.

The Cascade Lakes are 2038 feet above sea level and lie in another pass, there being just room for a stage road between them and Pitchoff Mountain, which would be a good name for the road as well. For seven months of the twelve there is a continual wrangle between the climate and the United States over this mail route. Whirlwinds of snow drift down from Pitchoff Mountain which topples overhead. Then the Government digs itself out. And repeat! The veteran stage driver, who says that he hasn't missed a trip for thirty years or killed a horse, is another of those sturdy Adirondackers of the old school, and a man to listen to.

The Cascades used to be called Long Pond and later Edmund Pond before the mountain divided them, Colden-Avalanche fashion. They are too cold and too small to make a very successful resort. But for bleak beauty they are to be flattered.

It is down-hill all the way to the Keene Valley, and from the top of the last and steepest hill even in lowering weather such as ours the view was widespread and soothing after the bleak, burned, roadsides of the long way we had come. Before us lay the most famous valley in the Adirondacks, the first settled, and the most beautiful still. Opposite, Hurricane Mountain rolled up into the mist; beneath, farm and woodlot and cottage sprinkled the valley floor. In June with a sun shining on the quilt of crops and trees, and the mountains curving high to the valley's rim there is no scene in the whole Park so charmingly comfortable and well set out. The best view of this valley, they tell us, is from the top of Hurricane —a philosophical climb for the Glenmore scholars.

Our destination was St. Hubert's in the upper valley. So with one admiring look at the huge elm opposite the Owl's Head, we ambled on. We passed comfortable cottages and broad fields and contented-looking people. Always before us the mountains closed together, running up into the clouds that deepened the impression of seclusion and great peace. We did not pause until we reached the store and, going through the village called Keene Valley, we crossed the Ausable. Here fortune took a hand and led us to Mr. Hale's.

Photo by Warwick S. Carpenter

KEENE VALLEY FROM KEENE HEIGHTS

We knocked for information as to where to pitch our tent. We stayed to converse. And we ended by camping on his sleeping porch. It was an admirable decision. The northeast storm drizzled on for a day or so, and we would have spent the time twittering with chill before a bedraggled fire. The cold rains of late autumn and the thaws of spring are the least desirable of all tenting weathers; a downright blizzard is far easier on the spirits. As it was, we helped our host poke birch-wood in the stove, helped Mrs. Hale out with disposing of the best cakes that ever griddled, and went to church with both of them. Life was a continuous party. Mr. Hale liked to hear of Luggins' exploits in the West. And Luggins enjoyed Mr. Hale's,—at least the bale of hay. It was Whipple and the Rev. Mathias who had first climbed along all the ridges, he told us. It was Perkins, the artist, who was on one of the Ausables with Old Mountain Phelps when he saw an unnamed mountain and said it had a Gothic look. The Gothics it has been called ever since. Old Mountain Phelps's widow was still living (she has just died). He told us how the otter, mink, and fisher must leave for warmer places about September 20 for he never saw their sign after that. He regaled us with accounts of deer hunts and bear hunts and of getting lost on Marcy when the night got "darker 'n a stack of black cats." He had often slept out in the woods with no blanket when the deer he had killed was too far to bring in. He had guided Charles Dudley Warner on his last visit. He told us about the other guides: how fine a man was George Beede. He showed us a verse about him, written by a Dr. Cumming in Stoddart's "Northern Monthly."

> Verde the genial and kindly,
> Verde the knight of the trail
> Wherever you're camping to-night, Verde,
> Here's a farewell and a hail.

In short, LeGrand Hale reviewed the golden age of the Adirondacks that has passed for us. Those must have been sumptuous days. When finally the sun shone on a frosty morning we were armed with diagrams and new enthusiasms for the trail.

Near the Hales, St. Hubert's Inn sits on a knoll in the eye of the most beautiful view in our land. I am aware of having used that superlative before; but this time I mean it. To the east the Giant of the Valley rises and rises. Before you Noon Mark tells the time. And toward the winter twilight stretches the upper valley, forested with splendid trees and flushed with the colors of the sunset sky sharp with Sabele and rugged with Sawtooth. The view over Raquette from our North Bay had given us enchanting bays and headlands. The prospect from the Lake Placid grounds had shone with Whiteface and the encircling ranges. This outlook from St. Hubert's does more with smaller means. It soothes while it uplifts the soul.

Our three-days' rain had been snow on Marcy, and Mr. Hale advised against the ascent. So at that time we did not climb the master peak. In fact it looked as if a premature winter was settling on the region, for on the day before Thanksgiving it snowed a foot in the valley. Until that and subsequent falls should have packed hard, any mountaineering would scarcely be worth the trouble. But Thanksgiving day was such a perfect specimen of calm winter that we determined to try the Giant. We borrowed some wood-going snowshoes, the round kind, and set the alarm for six.

It was just like Mr. Hale to be up and have eggs and coffee ready. Also as we were going out he poked two packages at us saying that if we ever got to the top, we might like a bite.

The trail was not hard to follow and at the difficult places a man who knew how to blaze (from the French, *blesser*, to wound) had written the way in capitals. Twice we came out on ledges that overlooked birthday-cake scenes. The snow was very light, but grew deeper and deeper—over two feet. I found it easier to wade and pull myself up the steepest places by little trees than to struggle with my webbed feet. The soldiers have cut a broad fire-guard along one section, which is as steep as a mansard roof. At length we topped the ridge. At once all the southern Adirondacks spread out below us. There was a thick grove of spruce to be pushed through, and we were at the top. The snow had been blown off. The trees below had caught it and some were almost buried. Frost flowers whitened their trunks. In the sun the sparkle was too blinding for eyes. And how the wind howled over the ridge!

From the Giant, Champlain looks fairly close. The view is not so comprehensive as from McIntyre—Wolf Jaws and the rest loom too high in the perspective. But a man would be greedy to want more. And he would be wise to climb out of season. There was a thrill in floundering through fairy-land not to be bought for less pains. And to slide down the mansard roof was worth all the exertion of getting up. Thanks to the lunch, which we ate at ten in the morning, our ascent of Giant was a huge success.

Of all the passes in the Adirondacks, Indian and Elk, Ausable and Opalescent Head, Avalanche, Onaluska, Caribou, Great Elba, and Ampersand Valley, the highest of all is Hunter's Pass, between Dix and Nipple, which leads you through a gloomy and savage country 3247 feet above tide level. From it another pair of these contrasted streams issues, the Schroon finding its way to the

THE GIANTS CLOTHED WITH STONE 291

Hudson, the Bouquet into Champlain. This gorge is only a couple of hours from St. Hubert's. And if you climb Dix, you get the variety of Adirondack shapes. Marcy is a dome; the Gothics a steep wedge tapering to a ridge; McIntyre almost a precipice on the southeast, and a long gradual slope from the northwest; Whiteface a peak, steep on both sides of the ridge; Sugarloaf a truncated cone, a sort of circular mesa; Dix itself a cone on a big base.

While you are looking out on the varied scene you realize how different are the two sorts of valleys in the Park. The one kind spreads out on a flat base with upstanding walls like a fiord as at Lower Ausable Lake or Wilmington Notch. The other belongs to the more conventional valley form, broader and with less abrupt sides, as the lower valley of the Ausable River and of the Raquette. The split of Mt. Colden and the Ausable Chasm is different from either.

From St. Hubert's Mr. Frank W. Freeborn was good enough to climb most of the mountains in summer with his watch in hand, and I am taking the liberty of appending his times, giving the minimum in each case. Hopkins Peak, 3175 feet, 2½ hours; Mt. Baxter, 2400 feet, 1½ hours; Noon Mark, 3550 feet, 1¾ hours; Mt. Colvin, 4074 feet, 2 hours; the Giant, 4622 feet, 2½ hours; Mt. Marcy, 5344 feet, two days. A very interesting account of these ascents by Mr. Freeborn was published in "Appalachia."

I have visited the Ausable Ponds in many weathers, but the most impressive was the first time there with Lynn. Snow flurries were drooping from the greater summits and sifting into the valley. The road led through a wood that was perfectly quiet, though on the sides of the mountains we could hear a gust tearing along from time to time. The road curved up through a fine forest of maple and birch and all the evergreens. At length we caught a glimpse of the white ice plain beneath us through the bare trees, and at the same time a staggering view of gloomy summits tossing the clouds between them. It was unexpectedly grand. That is the beautiful difference between this Park and Switzerland and British Columbia and the Yellowstone. In those classic haunts you expect to be swept off your feet at every turn by new magnificences, and you are often disappointed. In the Adirondacks you look forward to having the esthetic sense merely tickled from time to time. Consequently when you are confronted by savageries of bare rock and dignities of sweeping line, you discount nothing; you are hit by their full worth.

The distances of battle-ship gray, the hard blues of the cold cliffs, the swirling white of the frozen lake made a deep impression on us both. The snow had drifted high about the porch. Winter was established here beyond uprooting, while down home the school-boys were hoping hard for their first storm.

The mountains come down to the water's edge so abruptly that in summer the only passage is by boat. If you are coming from Marcy, you must arrange to have a boat meet you. We were safe on the ice. Our trail soon brought us to the Upper Ausable Pond, which in summer is a rendezvous for guides, but which we found as deserted as Eden after the fall. The view from this pond is less wild, but perhaps more beautiful than from the lower. Choice is a matter of personality. As you can have both, why decide? As you can settle on neither, don't decide! It makes relinquishing them easier.

The Ponds and the country about them are owned and protected by the Adirondack Mountain Reserve. This company has undertaken to preserve the waters and woods of their domain, to keep the streams in fish, to protect the game, and to render points of interest accessible by roads and trails to visitors. As this costs, the company charges, but moderately, and one is glad to pay for such obvious benefits. Boats on the lake, shelter overnight, guides for the climb, provisions—these are the wants which are foreseen.

The longer you stay at Keene Valley, the more

you take the mountains for granted, the more are you impressed by the less striking beauties. At first we almost ignored the Ausable. But its speed and persistent beauty, I find, swept a channel through my memory until I find it easier to recall in detail than the shape of Wolf Jaws. The waterfalls, too, are sights you climb to see with disdain, if you go at all. You have not heard of them and you expect little as the Keene Valley men are not great advertisers. But let me tell you that one stream on Marcy plunges one thousand feet into the dark Panther Gorge, that the Rainbow Falls spray color on the rocks in the early afternoon after its fall of one hundred and thirty feet, and that the Roaring Brook Falls comes down three hundred feet, leap by leap in the beautiful woods of the Giant. There are other cataracts and cascades along this valley and there are other beauties of hidden pools, of sudden prospects. The Panorama Bluff above the Upper Pond ranges half the great mountains for you in a splendid group. And as if these notable sights were not enough, Nature has carved one of those great stone faces on the cliffs of the Lower Pond to watch the lonely defiles through their slow change.

Photo by Warwick S. Carpenter

CROWN OF THE CLOUD-CLEAVER

CHAPTER XII

A CHAPTER OF ENDS AND ODDS

OUR leave of absence had now nearly expired. So had Luggins. The quantity of water that had fallen on his unsheltered hide was to him an astonishment and to us an anxiety. The exposure at Heart Pond had been bad for him, and it was well that our trip was finishing. But the thought of finishing hurt. A weight, unobtrusive at first, but demanding notice as the calendar turned the December sheet, settled on Lynn and myself. Of course we did not foresee the American declaration of war and Lynn's immediate enlistment; but we did realize that for six months we had followed a trail that we could never retrace. Other times, other trips, we told each other brusquely, and better ones. But we knew that there could never be a better.

Our intention had been to pursue the Ausable to its mouth, ending up with a view of the Chasm and then running for the train, eyes closed and never a look behind. But as the time to do it came, we discovered that both wanted something else. The Chasm was just a tourist sight anyway, and we had both seen Champlain. What we both secretly desired was to end up where we had begun. So we said good-by to the Hales, passed the turn-off to the Giant, keyed Luggins to a pace he had not attained for many a day, and set all sail for Euba Mills, Schroon River, Schroon Lake, and North Creek.

We were running away from the sight that Baedeker double-stars and pronounces the "most wonderful piece of rock formation to the east of the Rockies and should not be omitted by any traveler who comes within a reasonable distance of it."

The walled banks of the Ausable were once joined. Projections on one side, opposite like cavities on the other, prove this. Also the strata continue. The river has cut down to the ancient sea deposits, and you can find fossils of mussels and even the ripple marks imbedded.

You start in at the top after admiring the seventy foot Rainbow Falls, and after you walk about half the way, you can get into a boat and shoot the rapids. The dip of strata makes the ride even more exciting. The cliff rises to one hundred and seventy-five feet at one place where the stream is sixty feet deep and only twelve wide. The names attached to the carvings of the rock tell the whole story and sometimes more. They come in about this order:

A CHAPTER OF ENDS AND ODDS 299

                Rainbow Falls
      Pulpit Rock   Horseshoe Falls
      Lookout Point
    Boaz   Elbow
   Slide
    Pyramid   Stalactite Cave
  Plume   Devil's Oven
    Punch Bowl   Hell Gate
      Jacob's Well
       Mystic Gorge   Moses
        Long Gallery   Shady Gorge
        Point O' Rocks
          Smugglers Pass   Hyde's Cave
          Post-Office   Bixby's Grotto
         Point Surprise   Easy Chair
     Balcony   Flat Iron
    Shelf Rock   Table Rock
  Sentinel   Cathedral Rocks
  Broken Needle   Grand Flume
Pool   Sentry Box
                Basin

Not far from the chasm is the little gorge, Poke O'Moonshine, a name to lure one from the comforts of the grave.

But once having turned our faces home we stepped not to the right or left nor did we look behind. The way was downward for the most part, and after the mountains of St. Hubert's we had few eyes for the smiling, but uncommanding hillocks by the road. That night we pitched late and hurriedly beside the Schroon River, and before noon the next day had reached its lake.

The Schroon Lake country is comely, even in

December, and the lake, which is ten miles long, was smiling at us. For a fortnight we had seen nothing but ice on Colden, on the Cascades, and on the Ausable Ponds, so that the ripple of the waters not yet in hiding was a surprise to us. But we learned that the altitude was only about eight hundred feet. The lake was named after Madame de Maintenon, once Scarron.

Farmlands and woodlands alternated, and Marcy was already a shadow on the horizon behind us. Across the lake the peak of Pharaoh Mountain rose, but even if we had then known its wide outlook over a ten-leagued forest, I doubt if we should have made the wide detour. We were going home.

That night we chose our camp site with all the regard due last things. There was a stream called Trout Brook on the map, but even that magic word in no way betrayed half its loveliness and loneliness. The gods had sequestered it for their own fishing—and had forgotten it. A grove of hemlocks had been spared. The brook wandered past their roots. Ice had formed in its pools, but had not choked its little song, and we speculated to each other just how large a fish this sunken log harbored, just where we'd cast next spring to entice one from that ledge.

Before the sun had been drowned in a bank of ominous cloud in the southwest we had huge piles

A CHAPTER OF ENDS AND ODDS

of wood for defense. But no air stirred, and after supper a little fire, such as we had talked by half the summer evenings through, was enough for cheer and warmth.

In the heart of all mankind is the latent desire to live as we had been living. Subways, automats, elevators are easy, but they cannot quite stifle the call of the soil. A thousand years of starched collars cannot disestablish the memory of the hundred thousand with no collars at all. Vacations in the wild must be only vacations because civilization must go on. Orchestras would vanish and libraries molder back into tribal traditions if everybody took to the woods. Yet the woods will call us until we cut them all down and bury our heads in the sand to forget.

The talk that night was not of the park or new routes or even of Luggins. It resolutely kept off past pleasures as too much to bear, plumbing the future as best aid to the misery of a parting. It was late before we crawled into our blankets, and before I slept I heard that faintest sound, the scratch of snowflakes on the tent.

The morning found us in business mood. The snow was falling briskly, and there was much to be done. Luggins was glad to be moving, and we mingled no sentiment with our eggs. In two hours we were entering North Creek.

There was still much to be done: Luggins'

transportation and a merciful plague of details about getting off. Only as we sat in the train waiting for it to pull out did the contrast to our arrival well up into words. We laughed at our sensitiveness to the villagers' stares on that first morning when we cavalcaded along the road to North River, plodding Lynn, patient Luggins, and perspiring I. How we, had flaunted our independence incongruously in their faces! Then the buttercups had been bright along the banks, the bluebirds very blue upon the wires.

At last the train chugged out along the platform. We glanced out of the window. But the valley and its mountains were swallowed in the gray of the kindly snow.

CHAPTER XIII

WINTER PREFERRED

THOSE who have had their pleasure in calling America mercenary should bear in mind that it was the Swiss who first extorted dividends from winter. But let us not dispute. Now that we have discovered that we have a winter climate worth coining, let us have every one investing in boreal bonds and gilt-edge blizzards. There is no better interest offered. And the whole Arctic Zone goes security.

To witness our new-hatched enthusiasm an alien innocent might readily suppose that we had just invented the cycle of joys called winter sports. The truth of it is this, however. Winter sports began in America when the first dominie landed from the *Mayflower* and the first Pilgrim urchin planted a squshy snowball behind his ear.

From 1609 to 1906 winter sports were still in the urchin state. Throughout the Middle States, where you can never be sure of your snow, childhood *en masse* held unofficial prayer-meetings for the big storm, and when it came, constructed heart-breaking barrel-stave sleds and soap-box sleighs. Throughout the north, where you could be sure of snow if of nothing else, the urchinry took its pleasures unprayerfully and a trifle sadly as the season deepened and ravines had to be dug to the woodpile.

During this era of three hundred years the adult opinion of snow varied only in intensity. There was but one approved place for it and that place was particularly inappropriate for snow. And can you wonder? In the north for six months the stuff fell and accumulated until the most ambitious shoveling was necessary if burial was to be escaped. While to the southward, snow meant discomforts it would chagrin the devil to depict. And all this while, O shades of Yankee thrift! the high costs of snowing kept piling up without a cent's worth of return.

Then somebody went to Norway and discovered that the most exquisite sensation could be attained by jumping from the height of a third-story window, with some boards tied to your feet. Somebody else went to Switzerland and discovered that the most exhilarating feeling could be got by spiraling down a cliff and perspiraling up it again for the repeat. Finally, somebody else went to Scotland and discovered that the most exciting pastime in the (Scotch) world was throwing a cobblestone across the ice at somebody else with a broom. Thereupon these three discoverers re-

Photo by Warwick S. Carpenter

THE ORIGINAL WINTER SPORT

turned and roped off a mountain and charged admission to the next snow-storm. Thus began the winter sports of commerce in America; where they will end no one can hazard information. The Lake Placid Club spends about $20,000 a year now to enlarge and perfect its equipment. Saranac Lake and many another spot in the Adirondacks, the White Mountains, the Green Mountains, Maine, the West, not to particularize pioneer Canada, are investing solid sums in frost and flake. Shrewd capitalists have investigated winter and believe she has come to stay.

There is only one safe investment zone, however. It runs from middle Minnesota across northern Michigan, dips down into New York State, but not down so far as the southern end of Lake George, then bends north across upper Vermont and New Hampshire into Maine. The sub-depot of Old Man Winter is Essex County, New York, and his capital is the Lake Placid Club. The trustees of the capital have spent imperial fortunes to habilitate him in a manner worthy of a Prince of Hemispheres. And the P. of H. has done well by the trustees.

Winter in Essex County provides sleighing for about one hundred and fifty days. To go out day after day, relieved from the apprehension of a thaw, is an inconceivable sensation to one who has not lived in the far north. Winter is a bedraggled anxiety to a sports-lover unlucky enough to live between the Catskills and Point Discomfort. Each alternate snow-storm finishes in rain; furious cold is succeeded in a few hours by a warm fog; dazzling hopes are routed by drizzling despairs. A week of continuous sleighing is a boon, and two of them a portent. Even for most of New York State fifty days on runners is exceptional. So that the certain steady frost, the dry snow-cover that deepens week by week in the high country, is as gratifying as minstrelsy to the music-thirsty.

Winter at the capital is an enjoyment in itself. It would be enjoyable enough, just to recapture the careless thrill of childhood in snow-flight. But where nature, money, science, and daring have joyfully joined hands, the pleasures of sheerest speed are doubled. To participate in them is to wear the crown of clean living.

The three fundamental winter sports are sledding, skating, and sleighing. The three naturalized achievements are ski-ing, tobogganning, and snow-shoeing. The three exotics are curling, ski-joring, and ice-tennis. The three continuous extras are mountain-climbing, hockey, and snow-camping. And the great indoor sport is talking about it round the evening fire.

Sledding at the winter capital is tempered to one's courage. Gentle slopes on the golf grounds will lead you almost to the Ausable half a mile away. While if you are St. Michael and wish to tempt the dragon, try a flexible flyer on the toboggan chutes. The one in the woods was built on the thunder-bolt pattern: a downward plunge, a curve with the world falling from under, and then the long descent at Jove's own speed. It is glorious. But you must stay faithful to the hollowed track. One runner mounting to the softer edge, and you will dissipate your complexion if not break your neck. Sometimes I wonder when first in our race-history man threw himself to the winds for a sensation. How incongruously noble it seems to hazard a thousand chances for some peak, some northern pole, some moment of descent! How nobly unreasoning!

The Club is planning a great spiral run down Cobble Mountain for toboggans, and when the plans mature, remotest Switzerland will not be in the running. At present the four-track toboggan shuttle, which is to be supplemented by a nine-track through the woods, offers delight considerably safer than the sledding. Tobogganing is also more sociable than flexible flying. To race another toboggan is the sum of hilarity. To upset is to taste youth in the green. To get to the bottom is not the easiest amusement. The toboggans have been timed falling at the rate of sixty miles an hour.

Ski-ing gets the vote, I believe, because it is more godlike to fly erect than squatting. Again the risks are scaled to the prowess of the beginner. When the snow is too dry to cake and not too recently fallen, the littlest hill gives a fine momentum. To the novice it seems like dashing to destruction. Imagine then the rush from a forty-foot incline. You get a clear flight through the air of over a hundred feet. And as though a hundred feet were too infantile, nature has prepared a take-off from a hill so mathematically right that you can soar for world's records and yet not part too perilously far from earth. For the performer it is an encroachment upon the pleasures of the next world. And to the spectator it looks like a try-out for suicides. Yet beyond bruises and sprains there have been no injuries. And it is an egregious challenge to one's nerve. There stands the scaffold. They say it does n't hurt. Will you try it?

Ski-ing opens to you a new level of existence. It is good fun to fall and welter in fresh snow; it is better to glide carefully across slight hills; but to master the art of Mercury, to laugh in the dazzle of broad plains, to run through the beckoning wood, above the little trees and with no effort, is a new gift. It becomes clear now that we have taken life too gravely. Let us go lightly and sleep easier. And, indeed, when the day is through,

WINTER PREFERRED

and you sit before the heartening fire, and a delicious weariness creeps up your limbs and into your brain, and the whole world becomes a haze of comfort, you know that you have proved again the old formula you learned in the science class: for every action there is a reaction, opposite in effect, but equal in satisfaction. Ski-ing gives you a new kind of sleep.

Enthusiasts who are not content with the simpler forms of suicide try ski-joring. Ski-joring is engaging with the devil three to one. You set out to vanquish a horse and two skis. The result is a compound of intoxication and regret. But success does lay flattering unction to the soul, for it is no amateur accomplishment to master speed and a horse that seems depleted of good sense, to beat the devil on two feet of snow.

Ice-tennis is also a provocation wherein there is more than mirth that meets the ear.

Ice-boating needs a larger lake than Placid for any great interest. Saranac, Tupper, Long, Raquette, Cranberry would give the owners larger surfaces. It already is a favorite pastime on Raquette. But even there sixty miles an hour soon devours a six-mile reach.

Ice-hockey persists like an occupation at the winter capital. Even the Canadians come down to play. The Club spent much time and money in experimenting before they succeeded in making the best rink in our country. Tennis courts, side by side, flooded nightly in polar temperature and lighted by 8000 candle-power were the solution of the day-and-night problem. Hockey by experts is very much like the carousing of souls through space. When I shall be translated, possibly I may be able to vibrate like an electric whip-cord. But a good hockey-player does it in the flesh. He runs swallow-like on the steel blades, and his swoops are falcon-sure. But his pursuit of purpose makes him more than bird. There is no more ecstatic game to play, none more incredible to watch.

At the capital there is a space reserved for the curlers, and it is almost always in use. But only a Highland type-writer could do justice to the diversion, as I suppose it should be called. To curl properly you must have been raised on porridge and Scotch oaths. The game requires skill, strength, and all the other virtues except hilarity. From hearsay I had imagined it a pastime that the old fellows who somehow had outlasted cricket took to in their antiquity. But not so. You have to slam an immense stone of granite across a pond while your partner with a broom stands by. If the stone has not enough momentum, he sweeps like a chambermaid to speed it. And if it is going too fast he sweeps equally hard to hinder it. Then there is a celebration over the result that seems insufferably exaggerated until you think of golf.

There are twenty miles of ski-track through the capital woods; but there are twenty times that mileage of sleighing near by and fifty objectives to sleigh to. For companionship and easy comfort a sleigh knows no competitor, and Essex County as a sleighing ground challenges comparison with more famous fields. But the point is not in excelling; the planet is big enough for a thousand excellences. The point is always being wherever it abounds. Here are some pictures: the wind is blowing banners from white peaks, and spirals dance over the hills; great clouds of white sweep over the lake and across the plains; the horses walk, and the gale sings upon the telegraph wires. Or again: it is a road through the forest; the sunlight slants yellow underneath quiet trees; on the spruces lie piles of snow; the horse makes no noise; the runners make no noise; the snow is so soft and deep that it hushes thought. Or yet again: it is a night of full moon; the mountains rise about the broad valley, and the forests fall away from their white shoulders; the cold has a crystal purity; all space is spread out before us; only behind the spruces lies an unfathomable darkness; the speed of the horses is gratifying; after all, infinity is not what we most desire.

There are places where the ski, the toboggan,

and the sleigh cannot go, and there you'll need the snow-shoe. Snow-shoes may not be an invention of the devil, but certainly of an irreverent god. The sight of our divine form a-waddle is a spectacle for mirth. The first excursion, moreover, isn't likely to go better than the second, for by then you get adventurous. The shoes come loose. They come loose again. They trip you and get enmeshed in trees and rub you and come loose some more. After an hour of this you become acutely interested in the mileage home. But it's a handy knack to have. The long shoes for the plain, the round ones for the wood, and you can go anywhere in the white world except over precipices. It gives you a masterful sense to stump along with your duffle on a toboggan, knowing that no weather, no predicament of snow can embarrass your comfort. And it is the only way to get the view. I have climbed the Giant on six feet of snow in less time than I could have gone up in summer and been rewarded in a way that only winter landscapes know.

The deepest thrills run quietest, and I have purposely left to the last the supremest enjoyment of winter—the living in it. The only precaution one need take is to make sure of his winter, for by winter camping I do not mean the surprise by slush.

In the big woods there is actually less hardship

WHITEFACE IN NOVEMBER FROM COBBLE HILL

PHOTO BY IRVING L. STEDMAN

in winter than in summer. Let us count. There is no heat. There is no thirst. There are no insects. There is no wet. There are no spoiled provisions. There is cold, but five minutes' lively chopping after getting up will make you warm enough to cook breakfast. And you will probably wear only a shirt more than in the summer. At night you do have to be ingenious with fire, but it is possible. In winter, too, travel is only slightly more difficult, and you never have to carry a canoe. Also, if you climb, it is easier to find the way back to your camp again along the webbed trail than through summer moss.

In either case you do not go to the woods to escape hardship. You go for fish or freedom, for hunting or for health, and if I am not deceived as to your own character, you cannot help getting a lot of other things thrown in; growth and beauty, perhaps.

Probably there is no such thing as a scale of beauty; and certainly the winter woods are no more beautiful than the woods of spring or summer or fall. But they are an expansion, a new lane with many a curious turning. Few have tried this lane that leads to new adventures in the country of white enchantment. But those who have tried it come back clear-eyed and filled with wonder and delight.

CHAPTER XIV

WEATHERING THE WEATHER AND THE FLY

THE complexities of climate are revealed to the Adirondack voyageur in exuberant completeness. For specialties of wet and cold, drought and sunstroke, one may travel to special places; but to get all these at once in reasonable amounts one has but to remain within the boundaries of the Park. Nowhere else on our green globe, in the space of a week and without moving, can one enjoy weathers so ready, so entire, and so superlative.

For this reason any remarks that railroad folders and even more considered literature may make upon wardrobes and other anti-storm devices must remain inconclusive and perhaps idle. The severities of March so instantly succeed the tendernesses of May, the simplicities of Indian summer are so abruptly invaded by the contrariness of June, that one's preparation to be ample must be diversified beyond patience.

Yet, out of justice to an atmosphere that is so constantly being tried before our very petty juries,

THE WEATHER AND THE FLY

I must let the doctors witness to the fact that there is no more healthful climate to be encountered in this our playful vale of tears. Blizzards there are, and most amazing thunders, but there are whole days, too, of calm, and days of azure western winds and nights more delicious than draughts of spring water.

Taken all in all, the natives of the Adirondacks die only from over-feeding. There is no hay-fever at Adirondack altitudes; there are no colds; tuberculosis is checked; nerves quiet down, and insomnia is impossible. Good hours, good food, good society, and good air will rout the most accomplished doctor. Health soon comes to be the only complaint among those restless visitors who are under a sense of strain unless they have something to be under a sense of strain with.

And this miracle of change has been wrought by the admirable system of climatic excesses known as Adirondack weather. Unfortunately no wealth of data, no embarrassment of averages can quite foretell what atmospheric adventure one is to enjoy next. But there is a vague routine of conditions that one can set down without seeming entirely superstitious. As most campers arrive in early summer, I shall begin with that.

Summer in the Adirondacks is conservative. There is usually enough heat to draw attention to the season, but the achievements of the thermometer are not remarkable. Ninety degrees is never registered at Lake Placid and seldom at altitudes below fifteen hundred. However, I have seen villages that are far from water shimmer with heat like an able-bodied desert at midday. The nights in such places are always refreshing. No matter if the thermometer at noon is registering in the hundreds, before dawn you will be under one blanket and maybe two.

Of far more consequence to the tenter is the amount of rain, and it is just of this that the most unaffected liar fears to prophesy. July may be wet and August dry, or August wet after a dry July, or both may swim or swelter. One can rely on nothing but the certainty of excesses. Yet everybody lives through it. I have seen forty days of rain, a soggy wilderness, and moldering clothes bring a whole crowd of Christians into an ardor of execration, and yet they come up regularly to their meals, not missing once. I have seen forty days of drought, a woodland that crackles underfoot, and a sun that crackles overhead, and the same hardy crowd appearing thrice daily with the same bestial curiosity and without lapse. As Lynn explained once to a lady who could not get used to her shoes molding upon her feet, "Either you're ill or you're not ill. But you're not ill, so swamp life must be unmitigated wholesome." I think it was Lynn who was whole-

THE WEATHER AND THE FLY

some, really, for the lady remained well, despite the acknowledged insalubrity of swamps.

In summer there is one feature of the weather that baffles the plain mind. It is the ability of the mountains to shower. It rains from the east, of course, and from the south, but also from the west and other points. The rain balks at nothing when once fairly started. Whole regiments of showers troop over the ridges, and there is but one sign of their discontinuing: that is when the mists rise upon the mountains. No matter with what promise the day has begun, no matter if the wind blows from the usually sterling west, if mist gathers upon the mountain or gathered mists descend, there need be no misunderstanding: dull weather is certain. On the other hand, no matter how sullen or how low the clouds, if they but rise along the ridges, fair weather will not be long postponed.

July and August are the conventional months for camping, but they are not the best. Being the warmest, they permit more laziness as to night fires; but a fortnight of September will build one up faster than a whole month of summer. In September dark comes earlier, which is a disadvantage, but there are no clotted showers, no days of hazy heat, no insects. Rain it does, but rarely, and such days are followed by skies of deeper blue, air of a more delicious quality than ever July gave. Once or twice the mercury falls below the freezing point, and you have new intimacies with your fire. Midday is comfortably warm. The woods become almost articulate, so vivid are the colors. The summer crowd has gone. The inhabitants put away the tourist countenance and become again friends to speak with.

If September is the silvery month, October is the golden. Rains are cold now and are apt to end up in a spit of big flakes, and a shack is more convenient than a tent. But for whole weeks between storms the sun sifts through on the newfallen leaves, and the bear fattens on the beeches. The mercury shades off into the 'teens pretty regularly at a clear dawn, but the snows disappear in the next day's brilliance.

November may be anything that is no longer autumn and not yet winter. It is an unusual November that furnishes much sledding; yet there can be boreal onslaughts. Master Thomas's guide, Archie of the French blood, told me of being caught in a motor boat on Indian Lake when the big freeze blew down upon them November 24, 1916. The ice formed so rapidly that he was forced to land on an island and walk all night to keep alive. That night the government thermometer registered sixteen degrees below zero. November, then, ends the season for safe amateur exploits under canvas. The risks become

THE WEATHER AND THE FLY

too great. But the mountains never offer wider views.

With December comes the highland winter. The change is made overnight. Indian summer, which during November has lulled every one into a sense of perpetual peace, sometimes survives into the Christmas month. But suddenly the balance is overturned; the pent-up forces roll down from the north without dissimulation. The mercury drops impressively far below zero, at times to minus forty. About Lake Placid and on the western plateau, the snow falls to the depth of two or three feet. All wheels are changed to runners for three or four months. The Adirondacks of summer is lost beyond recollection. Only the outlines of the mountains remain, clearer, bluer, far more ethereal. To come upon Whiteface, soaring white against the blue, is to be exalted. A dazzling morning climb will kindle every honest sense that man possesses.

January and February show dark skies broken by tense brilliancies. The cold ranges from forty-five below to forty-five above, the commonest extremes being thirty and thirty. Almost always there comes a period of thaw to exaggerate the relapse. But only in exceptional winters does the ground uncover before March. And this security makes tenting once more possible. For with snow to bank the walls and a cold so dry that a shirt is overheating when you chop, there can be tasted pleasures of appetite, of exertion, and of sleep that lie beyond the range of comment.

March varies greatly with locality. On the higher levels snow falls throughout the month, while on the lower, the maple sap begins to run. The days, however, are long, and despite winter's hold and zero temperatures, the sunlight has a quality that is not long to be disregarded, and between blizzards icicles melt along the eaves.

Only with April comes disappointment. By now, you reason, you have deserved spring. But the storms are still of snow; drifts form higher than a horse's head along the cuts; the mercury still sinks to zero on abnormal mornings; the lakes are often unbroken sheets of snowy ice, unsafe for further sport and unsightly to one desiring spring. As the month advances, the change is sure to come. The lakes free themselves in a night. A red-winged blackbird appears along some shore; the robins come, and one day you hear the song-sparrow. Farmers seek their fields.

But even May can fool them. If it does warm up then, killing frosts are likely to come in June. It is best to give May over to cold and wet and let the frosts whiten on sodden turf at the beginning, for then there may be some hope of a reasonable spring before the end. For the average man May is no month to camp. On the other hand, one

A Home of the Old Wolf Days

Photo by Warwick S. Carpenter

THE WEATHER AND THE FLY 327

would be quite deficient if the pulse did not quicken at the smell of the warming woods, at the sight of the advancing miracle.

To be ready for June is to be ready for Paradise, if June herself is ready. For sometimes she is cold and drizzly. But even at the worst the birds are fully rehearsed, and the flowers will not be put off, and there is a softness in the skies and on the fluffy clouds that is the shining of the spirit of spring. When June is at its height, it is no longer an invitation. It is a command.

This climatological commentary has, I suppose, told little about the weather you will meet. Yet I doubt if facts or even angels could do more. You are welcome to the facts. The annual rainfall in the mountains comes to about 50 inches; New York City has 40. The annual mean of temperature ranges from Essex County's 36 degrees to 42 and 44 for the others; New York City's range is 50 to 54. It is a cold day that registers zero in New York, while 25 below is not unusual over all the mountain counties. In 1904 there was an official notice of −46. In the Adirondacks, frosts occur every month of the year, though rarely in July. In New York, May, June, July, August, September are frost-free, although outside of the city May 15 is a safer date to measure from.

But do not let extremes frighten you away. There are many compensating advantages. Vast reservoirs of ozone are at your service. The germs of colds expire from neglect and loneliness. Swift contrasts of storm and shine speed up your intellectual processes until legions of new brain cells are doing their bit. Greater storms, intenser cold, serener calms than more moderate climates produce, create undreamt-of beauties. And if it seems wet to you, remember that there must be some virtue in dampness or how should our Anglo-Saxon kinsfolk still endure?

The A B and Z of surviving weather is warmth. My hardy comrade and less hardy self found that we could get wet and stay wet with impunity as long as we kept our extremities warm. The chief danger to a camper is cold feet. Many times it rained off and on for a week. Fires were only of small good. They kept us cheerful, but it would have taken the resources of Satan himself to have dried out our quarters thoroughly. But socks, caps, even wristlets saved the day.

There were some other axioms that kept our courage up. A heavy thunder-storm in the woods is a great drama, and we wondered sometimes if the agencies were sufficiently rehearsed; so we said, "You will never see the flash that kills you." Sometimes it got uncomfortably cold in the autumn rain-storms, and Lynn used to say, "Well, if it gets much colder, it'll snow and make us comfortable." I recommend that thought. And once

THE WEATHER AND THE FLY

when we were in great danger from a squall, he paddled without a word until we were in the lee of a point; and only then I found that he had been in torture from cramp. Nerve like that, and commonsense, and a streak of humor will dominate worse tempests than those that sweep the Park.

There are but three things left, I believe, that the wit and fortitude of man have failed to harness for his good: weather, death, and bugs. We put up with the weather; we postpone death, but the insect problem beggars intellect. It is not exactly fair to lure an honest citizen to the North Woods without mention of the terror by night. A thousand may fall at his side and ten thousand by his right hand; yet by the prophets! there are a million to take their place! And judging by the bald head of a clergyman we once met by the roadside, there is no security for the godly in fly-time.

But I promise not to exaggerate. I can truthfully say that if a man is prepared, the pest of flies will make but negligible inroads upon his contentment.

The fly season opens with punkies about the middle of May, is augmented about June first by the black fly, and is further reinforced by the mosquito soon after. The black fly ceases to annoy by mid-August, the mosquito succumbs to old age or indigestion by the first of September or before, and the punky appears thereafter only on very propitiously close days. From June 15 till August 15 back in the woods or even on shore on sultry afternoons this triumvirate is likely to ruffle the calmest, but unless you've left your dope in camp, they never drive one to thoughts of self-extinction as they are reported to do in higher latitudes.

The affair, after all, is personal. I can only relate our impressions. We had a preference for the black fly because he gives you a sporting proposition. He attacks in numbers and he'll eat you behind your back, but with a patient accuracy on your part, you can avenge your blood. Whether it is gluttony or not, I have never determined. As Stewart Edward White says, "You can get him every time. In this is great, heart-lifting joy."

In the Adirondacks the black fly does not annoy you after twilight, rarely visits camp if it is put where it should be, and objects to the compound of sweet oil and citronella, half and half. This same dope was effectual for punkies also. The last week of June, which was hot and rather wet, we spent in the deepest woods, fishing. On three of those days the flies did not appear; on three they were bad. Frequent applications of the citronella gave us relief. And for the lunch hour a smudge kept us serene. The punky, however, despite his pin-point size, is no despicable antagonist. Why the Indians went to the trouble of kindling fires before which to torture their prisoner I cannot understand, when they had only to strip the poor man and turn on the punkies. If the punky were as large as a bee and kept his present ferocity, no one could remain a half hour in the woods. But he is not, by the benevolence of the Provider, and since the little beggar cannot swim in sweet oil, we are saved.

Not every smudge is successful. We kept a pail for the purpose, its bottom punctured for ventilation, into which we shoveled some coals from the cooking-fire and then scattered some moss or grass on top. This not only was portable, but perpetual. It would smolder an entire afternoon without replenishing and in its lee was safety. I know now why Brunhilde took such elaborate precautions.

The punky and the black fly are part of the woods. You accept them as you accept portages and the trout's day off, without oaths or bitterness. But the mosquito is different. It is an interloper. It observes no hours. It poisons the well it drinks from. And when you are on your back and at its mercy it gloats!

The Adirondack mosquito is not so plentiful as his Jersey swamp kindred, which in turn are relatively few, compared to the vast acreage of these creatures on the northern plains. Mr. White and

Mr. Seton have chapters descriptive of their concentrations that are as fascinating as a murder trial. But in the Adirondacks on a still July evening there are enough to make you give thanks for a mosquito-bar. Against him a smudge is doubtful defense and dope useless. Also, unless you are morally sure that your cage is perfect, you will not sleep. For that is the psychology of it. You are willing for him to grow apoplectic upon your carcass, but you resent the *te deum,* and you resent it to the extent of keeping awake to protect your property.

The day comes, however, when you realize that it is all over, that for some time past you have neither slapped nor sworn. For a moment you wonder. Then you appreciate what it means, and your heart beats once extra, and for the pleasure of this new immunity, two months of the sleepless little insect seems small pay.

CHAPTER XV

ON HERMITS AND OTHER TRAGEDIES

NOTHING could be nearer half a truth than to conceive of the Adirondacks as purely a pleasure land. The State owns about half of it and wishes all possible pleasure to be squeezed out of it that does not interfere with the serious offices of nature in growing wood, multiplying game, and toning down the climate.

The other half is divided up among lumber companies, private preserves, and small holdings, which are mostly very small.

A lumber company is a source of fortune to its stock-holders and a source of misfortune to everybody else. Nearly all of them follow the éstablished maxim of slash and sell out. It has paid in the past because it was so easy to move on to the next bit of primeval and repeat. But woods will not grow while you wait, and the stands of primeval forest that remain are about as rare as primeval heath hens—not all gone, but going.

Fire follows the ax, the injudicious ax, because of the heaps of slash, and taxes follow the fire because of flood and drought. There is nothing much left to follow the taxes except possibly one's peace of mind. This can be soothed only by the scientific hope that some backwoods inventor will bring out a substitute for newspaper pulp and the other common abuses of wood. So far that hope is transcendental rather than scientific.

While the lumberman is taking the clean cut to bankruptcy, the private preserve owner is, in many cases, administering his talent in accordance with strict forestry principles. Unfortunately on some estates, falsely called preserves, the most ruthless slashing is in progress. However, the great individual holdings are justified. If it had not been for them the forest preserve would have fallen into the hands of the rapacious. To-day they protect nearly a million acres, maintain woodlands that supply water and that are refuges for game. No work on the Adirondacks is quite complete without individual mention and description of these estates, some of which comprise the most striking of all the Adirondack attractions. But big changes are about to be made, so that it is necessary for the present to omit the names of the forty-odd private-preserve owners.

But to hasten on to the tragedies. The country embraced by the park and including the two great lakes to the east of it is not only a storehouse of legend, but also a complete outfitting establish-

How Doth the Hermit!

Photo by Warwick S. Carpenter

ON HERMITS AND OTHER TRAGEDIES

ment for the writer of chronicles. From it he can produce wars and raids and treaties enough to make any historian famous. It is an arsenal of colonial custom. But in addition to the Indian myth and the British redcoat there is a third layer of interest deposited on this fertile field for research—the story of business adventure. And some day a Gibbon or a Macaulay will investigate it and hold us spellbound with his tale of the ancient struggle to wrest riches from the wild beauty of the wilderness. A few specimen disappointments follow:

In 1792 an Alexander Macomb paid eightpence an acre for a bit of land containing 3,934,899 acres. He soon became insolvent.

The story of Brown's Tract—the John Brown for whom was named Brown University and not the John Brown of Ossawatomie—reads like a well-arranged tragedy with lurid catastrophes here and there to heighten interest. He is described as "a man of magnificent projects and extraordinary enterprise." He bought an enormous estate. He made roads which the frost destroyed. He built mills which rotted from disuse. He died leaving his lands still a wilderness. A Prussian son-in-law, Herreshoff, succeeded him. Herreshoff evidently had imbibed some of the old man's pertinacity. He declared, "I will settle this tract or settle myself." He did the latter with a pistol after he had run through all his own and his friends' money. Nat Foster, the famous trapper, slept in the old buildings until he shot an Indian and decided that he had better leave. His successor shot somebody else and drowned himself in Nick's Lake. Brown's Tract to-day is still mainly wilderness, and whoever wrote the fascinating report of the forest commission in 1893 summed up the whole affair in these words:

> The soil was none of the best, the climate was cold, the summers were short and the winters were long; the markets were distant and the roads to them were almost impassable during much of the year. One by one the settlers, growing weary of the undertaking, sold out their improvements or abandoned them and with their families left the forest hamlet to seek other homes. And now the old dwellings, with two or three exceptions, have disappeared; the school-house and its children are no longer to be seen; the fences are gone, and the once cleared fields have reverted to their original state.

Elsewhere I have told of Pierre Chassanis's attempted settlement of his half million acres and his consequent disasters.

The old dream of establishing a great estate on which to dispense hospitality in baronial style lured a James Watson to the Independence River. There he cut his throat.

Two men, Totten and Crossfield by name, outdid Macomb in the way of bargains, buying parts of Warren, Essex, Hamilton, and Herkimer counties, over a million acres, at threepence an acre.

ON HERMITS AND OTHER TRAGEDIES 339

Their associates, however, were strong for King George when the war broke out, and their land was seized.

And so the story goes. The wildness of the country allured; its hardships disillusioned. Army captains, who were given grants on the old military tract for repulsing hostile savages, could not work them. Sea captains tried to settle in the woods, one Chase saying that "he would rather have lost his right in Heaven than title to this soil." No matter how diverse the beginnings, the end was bankruptcy and discouragement, the chief variation resting in the manner of demise.

Baronial projects of colonial days were succeeded by better founded, but no more successful, schemes by corporations. Some of their remains still endure. It is not unusual to come upon some ruined foundry in mid-forest, a smelter for ores that could not be transported, a grist mill for grains that would not grow. Mr. Henderson of the Upper Adirondack Iron Works competes with Herreshoff of Brown's Tract for the biggest losses. Both began with iron and ended with lead, but they say that Mr. Henderson's shooting was accidental. There is one place on the property of the late mine owner where the Hudson flows over a dam of natural iron, and the whole country seems to be underlaid with rich deposits of magnetic ore. But the fifty-mile haul eats away all profit.

To-day it is out of the indirect resources that the inhabitants prosper. Garnet mines furnish much abrasive material, talc fifty thousand tons a year; there is marble in St. Lawrence county; gneisses and granite and Potsdam sandstone, lumber, game, and water-power, each yields its revenues. But neither farming nor lumbering nor mining nor ruthless slaughter of animals can return riches comparable to those given freely by thousands of men and women whose delight is the wilderness and its life. Not one extensive effort to subdue the wilderness has succeeded. But in every corner of it men who have taken it at its own terms are making a living, hard often, but not without its peculiar returns in health, honesty, and a certain freedom.

In every corner of it, too, have lived men who through a superior skill in their duties or through a marked personality have won distinction and remembrance. Many of these have been innkeepers like Paul Smith, Bartlett, Root. Many have been guides like Orson Phelps, George Beede, John Cheney. Some have been trappers like Nat Foster, some hermits like Jimmy O'Kane, some Indians. There is a great company of these silent men, memories for the most part now, who lived sturdily and died strong. Conditions are less rugged now, and so the rough hard-fibered school is passing. But the tradition of it will endure.

Of all the Indians, Mitchel Sabattis of Long Lake, pure-blooded, who died in 1906 at the age of ninety, is best known. A mountain is his monument. He spoke French, English, and two Indian dialects and told no lies in any of them. He collected the funds for the Long Lake church and was a very worthy man. In his day his skill as a guide was remarkable. He remembered having shot twenty moose, nine panthers, and any number of wolves.

Pezeeko was an old Indian who lived on his lake, now spelled Piseco. Sangermo was the hero of many stories of the North. Sabele's wigwam was pitched on Indian Lake as late as 1848.

Indians are getting scarce. But the hermit stays. A hermit is popularly regarded as an interesting failure. This, I suppose, is a revulsion of feeling from the old religious days when everybody who could get away from home ran off to the desert and slept on tacks. But, as somebody wickedly says, a man who sacrifices himself sacrifices everybody else first. And the families of the men who had gone off to mortify their flesh discovered that they were being mortified as well. So the hermit was made to feel unpopular. This threw him into a dilemma. If he returned to civilization, it would be a sign of weakness; if he stayed away, he would be abusing civilization. The status of hermits became delicate. And it has remained delicate, not to say one-sided. The world calls the hermit an interesting failure. The hermit would retort that the world is an uninteresting one—*would* retort but doesn't, because it isn't the hermit's rôle to retort. As soon as a hermit retorts, he ceases to be a hermit and becomes a normal being. Therefore we shall always be in darkness as to how a hermit regards himself. Thoreau's diary furnishes only relative information.

The hermits of the Adirondacks belonged to many categories. There was the draft-fugitive, the ex-bank-cashier, the refugee from sorrow. But those have gone. The Civil War conscripts have died, bank-cashiers are always caught now, and for my part I have never found anybody resembling those oppressed spirits of fiction, who are sequestered by romantic pens in the depth of the forest to brood over their griefs in silence and solitude. The hermits I have met have been kindly old men, relics who found it cheaper to live where board and lodging were to be had for the bother of pottering around. Some of them mutter to themselves, and their beards want washing, and the fences about their gardens are very rickety indeed. But they take time to eat, and have much to think about, and if they fail to put their thoughts down, how can you prove they haven't any? It is the writers who give themselves away.

CHAPTER XVI

THE SPIRIT OF THE PARK

THE spirit of the Adirondack Park is stated in the law that says that the land "shall be forever reserved and maintained for the use of the people." Every such statement, when backed up by enforcement, is a victory for democracy, and every victory for democracy is an advancement of the truest civilization. It is strange that we should have to go to the woods for the fulfilment of civilization. But it is very satisfactory and comforting.

As a nation we have got used to the idea of game refuges. Yellowstone Park is a success. We are just getting used to bird sanctuaries. Mrs. Sage and the Western States are seeing to that. But the notion of humanity preserves is fairly novel. We have our little air holes in the cities, which we call parks, and we have some sections of the West roped off by law which the East is welcome to roam over if it can pay the carfare to them. But it has remained for New York State to set aside more than a tithe of its total area

Photo by Dr. Edward L. Keffer

THE SPIRIT OF THE PARK

where men and women can seek sanctuary from cities and heat and the everlasting press of things. And New York State has done more. She has not only offered her mountains and lakes and woods to the tired student from Ithaca, the tired philosopher from the Hub, the tired business man from everywhere, but she has made trails through the mountains, has stocked the streams and lakes, and is doing her best to preserve the forest. The citizens of the State pay for this, and anybody can enjoy their gift for a thank-you. All that they request is care in the enjoyment. Great care is the least return that we can make.

The spirit of the Park is mutual forbearance for the common good. That should be the motto for the whole New World. Our ancestors came here for that very thing. Greed has made us forget at times. But in the Park once more there is scope to practise it, to begin again.

The rules of the Park are easy to imagine if you 've never seen them, easy to understand when you do see. They forbid everything that tends to damage the property belonging to somebody else. They encourage everything that does not interfere with the happiness of others. And the second column is much longer than the first.

The Park is not only open to America to visit, but her men and their families are invited to come and camp in it, to subsist on its fish, to enjoy its game under a liberal license. And there are but three major regulations:

The first asks the coöperation of all good sportsmen in preventing forest fires.

The second asks their rigid observance of the necessary game laws.

And the third requests the utmost care in avoiding the pollution of the water supply.

No thinking person can be blind to the lasting damage wrought by a forest fire. Yet unless it becomes the invariable rule of every camper, fisherman, and hunter to see that his match is out before he throws it down, to know that his cigarette is dead before he drops it, he will some day start a blaze. That man is not a good sportsman if he does n't carry water to pour over his fire before he leaves it, if only for an hour. It would make a raven weep to fly over some of the tracts of ruined forest that we saw.

A card to the Commission at Albany will bring the syllabus of laws relating to fish and game. A dollar will buy you the new map showing the lands belonging to the State, which amount to about fifty per cent. of the territory within the blue boundaries of the Park.

The rules about your tent are very simple. If the tent does not have a platform, you can pitch it anywhere not too near a spring without getting a license. If it has a platform, the Commis-

THE SPIRIT OF THE PARK

sion will grant you permission if you will inform them of the site desired. They will even reserve that site for you for the next year, though you may not do so without their annual consent. You may build a permanent camp if it is of the open kind, but it must only be used for reasonable periods. Portable canvas houses are allowed. You are not allowed to chop down trees, but you do not need to, for there is enough dead wood recently fallen to heat up Nova Zembla. The Commission will send you the "Circular of Information Relating to Lands and Forest" on request.

In this Park, then, you can squat, fancy free and fully fed, for months at a time. There are 600 miles of lake line to choose your camp site from. There are about 1450 lakes and ponds and nobody knows how many hills and mountains in the Park. You have about 4,000,000 acres to roam over within limits, and the average altitude is about 2000 feet, high enough for a change, not high enough to over-exhilarate. You have about 16 rivers to paddle on and thousands of little streams to fish in. There are about 50,000 deer to watch, and you won't be shot while watching them, for the law requires the hunter to see horns three inches long before he shoots. The woodcock, pheasants, ducks, quail are increasing. There are about forty kinds of quadrupeds you can set your restless children to observing; and when they know all those, there are a hundred varieties of birds. There are hundreds of miles of excellent motor road and dozens of good hotels; yet there are places still inaccessible except to those who are willing to undergo much toil for much pleasure. There are three great routes, each over a hundred miles long, two of them for canoe, that will prove the extent, the wildness, and the beauty of this Park which it is your privilege to enjoy.

The wisdom of the people in their outlay is only half told by the figures. But they are impressive. A million people reinforce their health there every year. The water supply for a still greater New York has been insured. Two million five hundred thousand horse-power, equivalent to an annual consumption of twenty-five million tons of coal, can be generated by the falling waters. But the best is the unfigured good.

I hope with a greedy energy that some day New York's sister commonwealths, though less richly endowed, will each set aside substantial amounts of their forest-land, their mountains, and their streams for human sanctuary. Each State contains desert hills, and hills not already turned into deserts, where reforestation is a crime to omit. Each of the Appalachian States could own some park whose streams might be stocked and whose woods and defiles might furnish camp sites for its people. And well they might. For that way gladness lies: in health and the exercise of liberty which is the spirit of all parks.

CHAPTER XVII

DUFFLE

ASCOT'S heart may be in the Highlands, but ours were in our duffle bags.

A duffle bag is a cylindrical bit of waterproofing in which your household gods are safe when it rains. Adam probably used one to remove his new wardrobe from Eden. But he didn't call it a duffle bag. It was first called that in the Adirondacks. The old Dutch traders took their beads and looking-glasses (made in Duffel, Holland) into the interior to trade off with the Mohawks for skins and real estate. Hence duffle bags.

When you go into the woods the contents of a duffle bag are useful and attractive. When you come out they are useful. Stern necessity has sifted them. It is the same with this chapter.

ACKNOWLEDGMENTS

I am hopelessly in debt. Before we went in our friends loaned us their wide knowledge of the Adirondack region. While we were in old guides and young guides, hotel-men and club-owners, fire-wardens and game-wardens, and even one highwayman, proved again the famous hospitality of the North Woods. Since coming out the librarians have done their bit. Therefore it would be a poor thing to mention just a few of the good-hearted people who offered us food or photographs or information or shelter or in one case, dear Mr. Hale, arctics. But those bits of duffle will always stay in our memory.

A PARTIAL BIBLIOGRAPHY

But the debt to authors can be more explicitly paid. I wish I owed to more. Indeed, the bibliography of the Adirondacks compared to that of the White Mountains is amazingly scant. It is made up of guide books, magazine articles, commission reports, and a few books.

Probably the most detailed guide is E. R. Wallace's which reached its sixth edition in 1878. S. R. Stoddart then came to the fore, continuing into the nineties. Then came Baedeker. But within the last three years new acquisitions by the State, new hotels, and the newest motors make a guide book pant to keep up with the changes.

The books of travel were written in the seventies and eighties when the wonder of this new territory was first breaking upon an astonished East. Mr. A. B. Street's accounts were enthusiastic enough. A Mr. Northrup took several excursions to the western plateau. Mr. N. B. Sylvester wrote graphic and historic chapters on the Adirondacks. Verplanck Colvin, though a surveyor, pictured the country with enthusiasm. Professor Emmons was its geological expert. J. R. Sims, Headley, the historian, Agassiz, Audubon, the "Personal Reminiscences" of Chittenden (pp. 139–168), all contain valuable references to the North Woods. B. J. Lossing wrote of the Dutch customs in his "Hudson from the Wilderness to the Sea," and John Burroughs has several references to enjoyments originating in those woods, notably in "Wake Robin" (pp. 77–108) and in "Locusts and Wild Honey" (pp. 167–196). Dr. Henry Van Dyke's account of his ascent of Ampersand in "Little Rivers" is told with an artist's accuracy and vividness. P. Deming published a book "Adirondack Stories," sad little folk tales.

There are several books, however, that have seized the spirit of the region and expressed it in living words. Murray's "Adventures in the Wilderness," Charles Dudley Warner's "Backlog Studies," Emerson's "Adirondacs," Dr. C. H. Merriam's "Adirondack Mammals," E. L. Trudeau's "Autobiography."

Trudeau's book is a gripping drama of a life-struggle, with its Saranac and St. Regis setting faithfully portrayed.

Merriam's "Mammals" is far more than a natural history. It is a loving account of the lives of the wild beasts that came under Dr. Merriam's observations of forty years.

The Emerson poem is best commented upon by W. J. Stillman in Chapter X of "The Autobiography of a Journalist." In other chapters Stillman tells about the Philosophers' Club and the effect of the woods-life on Emerson, Agassiz, Lowell. In straightforward and illuminating prose he gives a fascinating, reflective account of his months alone in the forest. One wishes there had been volumes instead of chapters.

Warner's "Backlog Studies" are always diverting and at times painfully ridiculous. When you read them the second time you realize how carefully mirrored is the Adirondack scene. His character study of Old Mountain Phelps gives you the most famous of the Keene Valley guides.

I have never read any of "Ned Buntline's" stories. He lived alone in a shack on Indian Point, Raquette Lake and wrote exciting tales.

The Rev. William Henry Harrison Murray, who should have been born in the Adirondacks but chose Guilford, Connecticut, instead, is credited with stirring up more interest in the Adirondacks than any other man. Verplanck Colvin rates high with his enthusiastic prophecies and tireless explorations. But Adirondack Murray has achieved the title "Father of the Adirondacks." He looked much like Mark Twain, and there was a lot of energy underneath his white hair. At the close of his life he was willing to go out and campaign for his beloved mountains when the Park seemed in danger. His "Honest John Plumley," the hero of the "Adventures," was a splendid old guide, and his naïve and moving tales will hold any boy or man either. See if you can help finishing "The Man Who Didn't Know Much."

If you can find old numbers of S. R. Stoddart's "Northern Monthly," you will be able to read intimate accounts of old guides, old habits, and old trails.

But for the Indians there is still no better man to turn to with a grain of salt than Cooper and, without the salt, Parkman. His pictures of the *coureurs de bois* and of the *bois* itself are finished. He wrote prose that took time to breathe. Would you not like to know the rest of this sentence: "Rude as he (*le coureur de bois*) was the voice of Nature may not always have been meaningless for one who—"

Many magazine articles have appeared in the last three decades, dealing with phases of Adirondack life, especially in "Outing." A periodical index will give them. But even more worth while investigating are the Reports of the New York Forest Commission. Some of its volumes are richly illustrated; in one or another of them

DUFFLE

every section of the Park is treated, and the reader will be surprised at the entertaining style in which they are written. The Adirondack region is so full of beauty, so rich in historical association that it is easy to believe that as a fountainhead of literature it will be of increasing value to American writers.

ADIRONDACK CENTERS

The Park can be seen superficially with a motor in two weeks. A month more would suffice for the two great canoe trips and a few climbs. But to know the region intimately, to know where you will find the trout, where you will see the deer, where the berries grow, to recognize the mountains as you would friends, takes years. On all counts the most satisfactory way is to take canvas or cottage at one of the centers and explore from it. Without aspiring to the thoroughness of a guide-book, the following scheme blocks out the chief centers with their neighborhoods. The center is in capitals.

I

Big Moose Brown's Tract
OLD FORGE Fulton Chain Raquette Lake Forked Lakes
Woodhull Lakes

II

Brandreth Preserve
Big Moose
Brown's Tract RAQUETTE LAKE Forked Lakes Long Lake
Fulton Chain Waubeek
Blue Mountain Lake Indian Lake
Kenwells

III

Raquette, Eagle   BLUE MOUNTAIN LAKE   Indian Lake
Blue Mountain

IV

Cedar River Country   Kunjamuk Country
          INDIAN LAKE   North Creek
West Canada Lakes   Jessup River
          Speculator district

V

Indian Lake

West Canada Lakes

         Jessup River
    SPECULATOR
   Lake Pleasant
  Sacandaga Lake
   Piseco Lake

VI

Tupper Lakes
                     The Saranacs
Raquette   Forked   LONG LAKE
                               Newcomb
  Blue Mountain

VII

Massawepie
                     The Saranacs
Cranberry Lake   BIG TUPPER LAKE
                        Raquette River
      Little Tupper

VIII

Oswegatchie River   Grasse River
     CRANBERRY LAKE
   Star Lake
Bonaparte   The Plains

DUFFLE 359

IX

Paul Smith's   Lake Placid
                    Upper Saranac
     LOWER SARANAC
The Tuppers   Middle Saranac
                 Ampersand

X

           Whiteface
Paul Smith's   Wilmington Notch
         Cobble
     LAKE PLACID
Upper Saranac   Cascade Lakes   Keene
     Heart Pond   Valley
    McIntyre-Marcy Range

XI

                 Chateaugay Lakes
                    Loon Lake
    Meacham Lake
               Osgood Pond
    Paul Smith's
   UPPER ST. REGIS
               Lake Placid
    Upper Saranac

XII

              Ausable Chasm
Lake Placid
    Cascade Lakes
Indian   Elizabethtown
     KEENE VALLEY
Pass   Marcy Range
       St. Hubert's   Champlain
    Ausable Ponds
Newcomb
    Schroon Lake

THE ADIRONDACKS

XIII

         Keene Valley
     Tahawus
   Newcomb
     SCHROON LAKE
  North Creek   Lake George
Indian Lake

AN AUTOMOBILE TRIP

The "Blue Book" with its consideration for tires, turnings, and tea-parties is not to be improved on. I can only add my humble word that Adirondack roads, except after an unusual downpour, are a matter for gratified surprise. Also they dry quickly. The usual routes are from Utica north, or along the eastern border. The road by Schroon Lake is magnificent. But if I were showing off the mountains, I would begin at Northville, southern boundary of the Park, run through the beautifully wooded section to Speculator, then go north and along the west shore of Indian Lake to Blue Mountain Lake, take a day off for the boat trip to Raquette, then motor by Long Lake, skirt the big mountains to the south, passing through Newcomb, Tahawus, turning north to Elizabethtown, from which it is a charming hour to Keene Valley, which should be ascended to St. Hubert's. Then the route would be down the Ausable to the Forks and up through the Wilmington Notch to Lake Placid, Saranac, and Paul Smith's. But not even a twin-sixty can show you all the Adirondacks.

A WALKING TRIP

The walker has still the last laugh. He can point to many a place in the Park where neither paddle nor gasoline nor horse flesh can go. And the secret of a good walking trip is finding just such places, for footing it in the dust of vehicles somewhat dims the adventure. In an Adirondack pack basket you can carry one blanket and a little food, which with a compass, a little money, and good shoes—but let us not start an argument as to the order of going. The destination, I should say, is Essex County. West of the railroad it is difficult and monotonous for pleasure-walking. The Cedar River country is too wild for going light. The Schroon Lake region is too mild. The Raquette and Saranac sections are better for a canoe. For a specimen good time how is this?

First day.	Leave train at Westport. Walk to Keene Valley, 24 miles, easy road.
Second day.	Climb Giant for view of southeast of Park.
Third day.	Loaf and enjoy the Ausable Ponds. Sleep on Upper.
Fourth day.	Climb Marcy, descending by Colden to the Iron Works.
Fifth day.	Exploration of the Gorge of the Opalescent.
Sixth day.	Leisurely trip over Indian Pass to Heart Pond.
Seventh Day.	Hallow it. (Cf. Wordsworth or Thanatopsis.)
Eighth day.	Climb McIntyre for the 135 lakes.

Ninth day.   John Brown's farm, Lake Placid, and a hot bath, 8 miles.
Tenth day.   Climb Whiteface for view of Montreal and points north.

TWO HUNDRED-MILE CANOE TRIPS

The Adirondack Park probably furnishes the most satisfactory canoe touring in our country. The following chart shows only some of the possibilities. I have written *draw* for carries made with a horse:

FULTON CHAIN

First Lake	1½ miles
Second Lake	1 mile
Third Lake	1 mile
Inlet	40 rods
Fourth Lake	6 miles
Fifth Lake	¼ mile
Carry	¾ mile
Sixth Lake	½ mile
Inlet	1 mile
Seventh Lake	2 miles
Inlet	1¼ miles
Draw	1 mile
Eighth Lake	1¾ miles
Draw	1¼ miles
Brown's Tract Inlet	4 miles

RAQUETTE LAKE

TO Mouth of Marion River	3½ miles
Marion River to Carry	4 miles
R. R. Carry	½ mile
Utowana Lake	2 miles
Inlet	½ mile
Eagle Lake	1 mile

DUFFLE

BLUE MOUNTAIN LAKE

OR TO Forked Lake Carry	9	miles
Carry	½	mile
Forked Lake	3	miles
Draw	1½	miles
River	short distance	
Carry about Buttermilk Falls	a few rods	
River	4	miles
Carry	½	mile
River and soon		

LONG LAKE .... 14 miles

Raquette River	6	miles
Draw	1½	miles
River	6	miles
Draw to Upper Saranac	2	miles
Saranac Inn	9	miles
Draw to Big Clear Pond	3	miles
Big Clear Pond	2	miles
St. Germain Draw	1½	miles
Upper St. Regis	1	mile
Spitfire	1	mile
Inlet Lower St. Regis (Paul Smith's)	1	mile
Draw to Osgood Pond	1	mile
Osgood Pond	2½	miles
Inlet	1	mile
Lucretia Lake	1½	miles
Short Carry Rainbow Lake	3	miles
Lily Pad Pond		
Lake Kushaqua	5	miles
Mud Pond		
Carry	1	mile

LOON LAKE about 102 miles from Blue Mt. and about 115 from Old Forge.

OR

Instead of going from Upper Saranac to Paul Smith's one can go to

Outlet (from Indian Carry)	2	miles
Carry around dam		
River	½	mile
Middle Saranac	3	miles
Stream (with carry)	3	miles
Lower Saranac to village	6	miles

OR

Instead of deviating into the Saranacs on the way from Long Lake, keep on

Raquette River to Big Tupper	21	miles
Bog River	1	mile

(or the Bog may be ascended into its marshy lakes)

Draw to Round Pond	2	miles
Round Pond	2	miles
Inlet	1	mile
Little Tupper	6	miles

(From here five little carries with ponds intervening will bring you out on Little Forked and so to Raquette.)

Doubtful stream to Charley Pond	3	miles
Charley's Pond	¾	mile

Inlet.

(Deer Pond, Little Rock, West, Shingle Shanty Ponds make too big a tangle, so)

Carry to Lake Lila	2	miles
Lake Lila	3	miles
Outlet to Lake Nehasane	3	miles
Lake Nehasane	4	miles

Carry down outlet .... ¾ mile
Beaver River to Stillwater .... 25 miles

This route totals about 105 miles from Saranac Village.

SOME CLIMBS

One of the prime methods of self-deception is to decide on a climb because of its measurements. Beauty never was expressed in feet above sea level, and reward in the matter of view suspends all moral laws by declining to bear any relation to the labor involved. Twenty minutes up little Cobble does more for you than a two-hours' sweat up Dug Mountain. Still, a few representative heights are interesting:

Marcy (5344 feet) gives a survey of the entire Adirondacks, but makes most of the mountains look like a cluster of haycocks.
Whiteface (4871) is isolated, shows Ontario, the St. Lawrence and a magnificent circle of horizon.
McIntyre (5112) shows the maximum number of lakes.
The Gothics (4744) is the heart of the great range.
West Mountain (2919) gives a near view of the lake country.
Snowy (3903) gives an impressive expanse of forest cover.
Speculator (3041) shows the southern districts.
Gore (3539) shows the valley of the Hudson.
Blue (3762) is for a central viewpoint.
Ampersand (3432) gives what Dr. Henry Van Dyke considers the finest view of all.

Haystack (4918)	Noon Mark (3550)	Giant (4530)
Dix (4916)	Cobble (1936)	Hurricane (3763)
Colden (4753)	Seward (4384)	Santanoni (4644)

THE BOTTOM OF THE BAG

When is a duffle bag ever absolutely full—or empty? There were lots of things that Lynn and I missed—multitudes of lakes, some of the rivers, several of the fish. We did n't know enough to look for the Military Road that was built for the War of 1812, or to visit the great falls of the Ausable, or to look for Indian arrow-heads and graves on the shores of Raquette, or to see the huge moraine between Blue Mountain and Cedar river. We did n't realize that there are a dozen kinds of conifers to look for, or that most of the flat meadows were due to beaver, Indian Clearing containing one thousand acres underlaid with peat, or that evergreen air is not only aseptic, but antiseptic. For those we shall go again.

But there is one thing we did not miss. It goes with the duffle that has seen much strain and wear—the sense of fellowship for those bent on the same errand of enjoying the woods. And when one day we found in Adirondack Murray a frank expression of that very thing, Lynn said, "That 's a smooth thing to beach your book on." So here it is:

"For if you but love the out-door life as I do love it you are friends to me, even kith and kin, by a relationship finer and closer than that of blood—likeness of nature."

INDEX

Acknowledgments, 352
Adirondack, 273
Adirondack altitudes, 365
  ascents, 291
  centers, 357
  Forest Preserve, 16
  geology, 15
  hermits, 341
  Lodge, 262
  Mt. Reserve, 293
  mountain shapes, 241
  Park resources, 349
  Park rules, 348
  Park dimensions, 23
  passes, 290
  Plateau, 147
  seasons, 319
  trips, 360
"Adirondack" Murray, 15, 355, 366
"The Adirondacs," 224
Agassiz, 224
Ampersand, 223, 230
Association for Preservation of the Adirondacks, 97
Ausable chasm, 298
  ponds, 292
  River, 294
Avalanche Lake, 277
Axton, 129

Balsam, the, 86
Bear, the, 180
Beaver, the, 188
Beavertown, 221
Beech, the, 91
Bibliography, 353
Big Tupper Lake, 137
Big Simon's Pond, 134
Birches, the, 87
Black fly, the, 330
Black River, 221
Blue Mt. Lake, 108
Bonaparte, Joseph, 222
Botheration Flow, 37
Brandreth Brook, 114
Brandy Brook, 169
Brown, John, 259
Brown's Tract, 337
Brown's Tract Inlet, 119
Butter Brook, 73
Buttermilk Falls, 124

Calamity Pond, 277
Canada Creek, 50
Canoe trips, 362
Cascade Lakes, 283
Cedar River, 66
Champlain, Sieur de, 9
Chateaugay Lakes, 229
Chazy Lake, 229
Childwold, 157
Chimney Mt., 40
Climbs, 365
Colvin, Verplanck, 14, 97
Conifer, 170
Corinth, 13
Crags, the, 104

Cranberry Lake, 157
Crotched Pond, 60
Curling, 312

Diana, 222
Deer, the, 182
Dewey, Melvil, 240
Dix Mt., 291
Dug Mt., 47, 56

Eagle Lake, 108
Elk, the, 180
Emerson, 224

First settlements, 10
First summer boarders, 13
Forestport, 13
Forked Lake, 124, 142
Fox, the, 197
Fulton Chain, 117, 362

Garnet mine, 34
Giant-of-the-Valley, 289
Glacial period, 6
Gore Mt., 37
Gothics, the, 287
Grasse River, 169
Guides, 14, 37, 168

Hanging Spear Falls, 278
Heart Pond, 261
Hemlock, the, 85
Herreshoff, 337
Hinckley, 13
Hough, 15
Hour Pond, 34
Hudson River, 28, 33
Hunters' Pass, 290
Hurricane Mt., 284

Ice-boating, 311

Indian Face, 294
Indian Lake, 48, 58
Indian Pass, 268
Inhabitants, Dutch, 11
  French, 12, 221
  Indian, 7, 341
  Irish, 12
  Scotch, 12
Iroquois Ravine, 268

Jessup River, 58
John Mack Pond, 60

Keene Valley, 284 ff.
Kenwells, 163
King's Flow, 39
Kunjamuk, 37, 39, 43, 59

La Compagnie de New York, 221
Lake Bonaparte, 222
Lake Colden, 278
Lake Henderson, 272
Lake Lila, 149
Lake Massawepie, 172
Lake Placid, 238
Lake Placid Club, 240
Lake Pleasant, 49
Lewey Lake, 59
Little Moose Lake, 69
Long Lake, 127
Loon Lake, 229
Lost, 67
Lowell, 224
Lucretia Lake, 227
Luggins, explained, 29, 159
  admired, 58
  reproached, 231
Lynx, the, 179

Macomb's Purchase, 337
Maple, the, 88

INDEX

Maple sugar, 88
Marion River, 107
Mason Lake, 58
Miami River, 58
Mice, the, 201
Miller, Mr. Wm. J., 40
Mink, the, 203
Modes of travel, 29
Moose, the, 179
Mosquito, the, 331
Mount Colden, 278
Mount McIntyre, 279
Mount Marcy, 59, 280
Mount Morris, 134
Mount Jo, 267
Mount Seward, 281
Murray, Adirondack, 15, 355, 366

Nameless Creek, 119
Nat Foster, 338
Natural Bridge, 223
Nehasane Park, 149
Niggerhead Mt., 104
Noon Mark, 288
North Creek, 27, 301
North River, 28

Old Forge, 118
Opalescent River, 277
Osgood Pond, 227
Oswegatchie River, 163
Otter, the, 203
Otter Brook, 75

Panorama Bluff, 294
Panther, the, 178
Panther Gorge, 294
Peaked Mt., 33
Pezeeko, 341
Pharaoh Mt., 300

Phelps, Old Mountain, 240, 287
Philosopher's Club, 224
Pine, the, 84
Piseco Lake, 50
Pitchoff Mt., 283
Poke o' Moonshine, 299
Porcupine, the, 191
Primeval forest, 80
Preston Ponds, 277
Punky, the, 331

Raccoon, the, 200
Rainbow Falls, 294, 298
Rainbow Lake, 228
Raquette Lake, 103
Raquette River, 123
Remsen, 18
Roaring Brook Falls, 294
Round Trip, the, 227

St. Hubert's, 288
Sabattis, 341
Sabele, 288, 341
Sacandaga Lake, 50
Sangermo, 341
Saranac Lake, Upper, 129
Saranac Lake Village, 230
Sawteeth, 288
Schenectady, 10
Schroon Lake, 299
Shallow Pond, 119
Silver Brook, 73
Ski-ing, 310
Ski-joring, 311
Sledding, 308
Sleighing, 313
Smith, Paul, 210
Snow-cave, 42
Snow-shoeing, 314
Snowy Mt., 60
Speculator, 48

Spruce, the, 86
Squaw Brook, 65
Star Lake, 164
Stevenson, 219
Stillman, 224
Sweeney's Carry, 133

Tahawus, 59, 280
Tahawus Club, 273
Tear of the Clouds, 277
Thirteenth Lake, 29
Tobogganing, 309
Totten and Crossfield's Purchase, 338
Trudeau, Dr. E. L., 214

Utica, 10

Utowana Lake, 108

Walking trip, 361
Wall Face, 270
Wanakena, 162
Weasel, the, 203
Weather statistics, 327
West Mt., 113
Whiteface Mt., 281, 323
Whitney Preserve, 140
Whittaker Lake, 48, 52, 56
Wild-cat, the, 179
Wilmington Notch, 234
Winter camping, 314
Wolf, the, 177
Wood-chuck, the, 198